Lecture Notes of the Institute for Computer Sciences, Social Informatics and Telecommunications Engineering 575

The LNICST series publishes ICST's conferences, symposia and workshops.
LNICST reports state-of-the-art results in areas related to the scope of the Institute.
The type of material published includes

- Proceedings (published in time for the respective event)
- Other edited monographs (such as project reports or invited volumes)

LNICST topics span the following areas:

- General Computer Science
- E-Economy
- E-Medicine
- Knowledge Management
- Multimedia
- Operations, Management and Policy
- Social Informatics
- Systems

David Crawford · Jeremy Foss ·
Nicholas Lambert · Martin Reed · Jennah Kriebel
Editors

Technology, Innovation, Entrepreneurship and Education

4th EAI International Conference, TIE 2023
Cambridge, UK, September 27–28, 2023
Proceedings

 Springer

Editors
David Crawford
Ravensbourne University London
London, UK

Nicholas Lambert
University of South Wales
Cardiff, UK

Jennah Kriebel
Harvard College
Cambridge, MA, USA

Jeremy Foss
Birmingham City University
Birmingham, UK

Martin Reed
University of Essex
Essex, UK

ISSN 1867-8211 ISSN 1867-822X (electronic)
Lecture Notes of the Institute for Computer Sciences, Social Informatics
and Telecommunications Engineering
ISBN 978-3-031-59382-6 ISBN 978-3-031-59383-3 (eBook)
https://doi.org/10.1007/978-3-031-59383-3

This Springer imprint is published by the registered company Springer Nature Switzerland AG
The registered company address is: Gewerbestrasse 11, 6330 Cham, Switzerland

If disposing of this product, please recycle the paper.

Preface

I am delighted to introduce these proceedings for the EAI International Conference on Technology, Innovation, Entrepreneurship and Education (TIE 2023), held at Magdalene College, Cambridge on 27th and 28th September 2023. This radical conference attracted attendees from around the world, with a programme of cutting-edge presentations showcasing the latest technical, business and pedagogic innovations. Conference delegates learned of exciting new connections and opportunities that exist within the conference's four 'knowledge pillars' of Technology, Innovation, Entrepreneurship and Education. The conference informed delegates of how new ideas in these critical areas can be guided along the path to success in this fast-moving era of Virtual Worlds and Artificial Intelligence.

The programme of papers and presentations at TIE 2023 divided into two streams:

- main track, comprising formal papers to explain in some detail how innovative ideas, techniques and new technologies (like virtual reality experiences and computer game platforms) can be introduced advantageously into teaching programmes in schools and higher education institutions.
- demos & workshop track, made up of a series of short presentations and hands-on demonstrations, showcasing how inventors can turn ideas into business reality; and how new technologies create opportunities in the education and entertainment sectors.

These proceedings and my introduction will cover only the formal papers from the conference main track stream. However, in future years we may consider publishing also a synopsis of the Demos & Workshop presentations, as they provide an informal but informative glimpse of future technologies and applications.

The TIE 2023 conference main track programme covered four discrete areas: International School Projects; Technology in Education; Technology for Content Creation; and Future Content Delivery. In addition to the high-quality paper presentations in these sessions, the conference was honoured to be supported by three eminent Keynote addresses particularly relevant to its themes from: Phil O'Donovan, from the "Cambridge Angels" start-up funding organisation; Alex Chung, founder and CEO of the successful US start-up company "Giphy"; and Shafi Ahmed, surgeon and "Metaverse Medtech" guru. Due to time constraints, the conference main track papers programme was limited to 10 formal papers; and we are pleased to publish these papers in this volume for your edification.

The success of TIE 2023 was undoubtedly due to the commitment and support from all the committee members. I am deeply indebted to the diligent labours of the Program Chairs: Jeremy Foss, Birmingham City University; Nick Lambert, University of South Wales; and Martin Reed, University of Essex. It was also a great pleasure to work with such an excellent organising committee team, organising and crafting the conference programme so successfully. In particular, I commend: Jennah Kriebel; Ingeborg Albert; John Emmett; Barry Tew; Lawrence Lartey of Ravensbourne University London; Rachel Kerr of Cambridge Wireless; Adeboye Dada of University of Northampton; and Femi

Adeyemi-Ejeye of University of Surrey. I would also like to thank sincerely: Ivana Budjakova, EAI Conference Manager, and Radka Vasileiadis, EAI Head of Conferences, for their guidance and steadfast resolve; and the Sports Video Group (Europe) for their generous sponsorship for five student attendees.

September 2023

David Crawford
Jeremy Foss
Nicholas Lambert
Martin Reed
Jennah Kriebel

Organization

Organizing Committee

General Chair

David Crawford — Ravensbourne University London & University of Essex, UK

General Co-chairs

Jeremy Foss — Birmingham City University, UK
Nick Lambert — Startup Stiwdio Sefydlyu, University of South Wales, UK
Martin Reed — University of Essex, UK

TPC Chairs and Co-chairs

Lawrence Lartey — Ravensbourne University London, UK
Ingeborg Albert — independent

Local Chair

Rachel Kerr — Cambridge Wireless, UK

Workshops Chair

James Marks — PlayLa.bZ, UK

Panels Chair

Jennah Kriebel — UN Women, Switzerland

Demos Chair

Nadia Aziz — Unbounded Future Ltd, UK

Technical Program Committee

Adeboye Dada	University of Northampton, UK
Femi Adeyemi-Ejeye	University of Surrey, UK
Szczepan Orlowski	Animorph Co-op, UK
Jenny Young	Anglia Ruskin University, UK
Muriel Deschanel	B-com SARL, France
Meghna Chhabra	Delhi School of Business, India
Lawrence Murphy	University of Salford, UK
Nadia Aziz	Unbounded Future Ltd, UK

Contents

Future Content Delivery

International School Projects

Predicting School Dropout in Malawi

Mudaniso Hara[1]($\boxtimes$), Amelia Taylor[2], and Precious Gawanani[1] ⓘ

[1] Lilongwe University of Agriculture and Natural Resources, Lilongwe, Malawi
{mhara,pgawanani}@luanar.ac.mw
[2] Malawi University of Business and Applied Sciences, Blantyre, Malawi
ataylor@mubas.ac.mw

Abstract. School dropout is a significant issue, especially in developing countries due to high poverty levels and inadequate allocation of resources to education. This study applies Machine Learning to predict dropouts in the Lilongwe University of Agriculture and Natural Resources' open and distance education system. Four supervised machine learning classifiers (Gaussian Naïve Bayes, Logistic Regression, K-Nearest Neighbour, and Random Forest) were assessed to find the best predictor for dropouts. Data imbalance was addressed using oversampling and undersampling techniques. Results showed that Random Forest performed the best with under-sampling. Hyperparameter optimization using grid and random search methods also improved performance, with Random Forest emerging as the best classifier. This study contributes to future research and enhances the existing literature. It is expected to improve student support services by proactively addressing at-risk students, reducing attrition rates.

Keywords: school dropouts · machine learning · hyperparameter optimisation

Acronyms

AUC Area Under Curve. 7, 9, 10
HPO Hyperparameter Optimisation. 10, 11
KNN K-Nearest Neighbours. 7, 9
LR Logistic Regression. 7, 9, 10
LUANAR Lilongwe University of Agriculture and Natural Resources. 3, 4, 11
ML Machine Learning. 2, 11
NB Naive Bayes. 7, 9
ODL Open and Distance Learning. 2, 4, 11
RF Random Forest. 7, 9–11
RUS Random Under-Sampling. 8–11
SMOTE Synthetic Minority Oversampling Technique. 8, 10, 11

Supported by LUANAR/MUBAS.

D. Crawford et al. (Eds.): TIE 2023, LNICST 575, pp. 3–16, 2024.
https://doi.org/10.1007/978-3-031-59383-3_1

1   Introduction

Access to higher education remains a challenge in Malawi. In 2010, the country had only 64 higher education students per 100,000 inhabitants [3]. The gross enrolement rate in tertiary education was 0.8% for both males and females in 2008. [4]. During the 2018/2019 public university selection process, only 23% of the eligible candidates (5,599 out of 24,583) were selected [9]. Despite the government's policy change in 2009 to increase admissions, universities have had to adopt Open and Distance Learning (ODL) programs to enhance access to higher education. However, challenges persist in implementing ODL, such as delayed feedback, prolonged semesters, lack of course information, and inadequate student support which have led to an increase in the number of school dropouts amongst ODL students [4].

Current studies on school dropout in Malawi primarily analyze past records and focus on identifying challenges and causes after dropout has occurred [3,5,6,13–15]. This approach overlooks the opportunity to identify at-risk students using factors such as academic performance, course grades, demographics, and pre-admission records. Universities in Malawi require effective solutions that can proactively address dropout by enabling early interventions and engaging students at risk. In Sub-Saharan Africa literature that looks at the application of Machine Learning (ML) in predicting student's dropout remains scanty as compared to developed countries [10]. In countries, such as Kenya, Tanzania, South Africa, Nigeria, and Ghana some studies exist [1,8,10–12,16,18]. However, studies have revealed that data are a challenge in most cases when it comes to conducting educational related studies in developing African countries. According to [10–12], in many sub-Saharan African primary and secondary schools, records management is predominantly manual, resulting in data gaps. Additionally, the lack of publicly accessible repositories poses a challenge in terms of data availability. Machine learning models have shown promising results in various studies related to school dropout and can potentially offer valuable insights in this context as well [2,7,10–12,16]. Such solutions do not exist in Malawian schools. It is therefore this gap that has prompted this study to develop a machine learning based school dropout predictive model that could predict dropouts before they happen to allow early interventions. Malawian universities are adopting learning management systems (LMS) to track students' academic records, including preadmission records. This improves record organization compared to lower educational levels. These records encompass academic grades, preadmission school grades, withdrawal history, disability status, and demographics. Access to such data presents an opportunity for applying ML predictive modeling. A case study conducted at Tshwane University of Technology in South Africa used a dataset of 4419 student records from the institution's database to identify at-risk students for dropout [8]. ML has proved to be one of the well sought solutions of addressing this student attrition problem as shown by other similar research [2,7,11,12,16].

2   Objectives and Methods

The main objective of this study was to predict school dropouts through application of machine learning. We take the case study of the LUANAR ODL system. We analysed data from the university's Students Academic Registration System (SARIS) collected over from 2016 to 2021.

We applied several classifiers to predict student dropout on selected features. The classifier performance was evaluated and the best classifier was further fine tuned using hyperparameter optimization approach. The aim was to provide a data-driven solution in forecasting students at risk of school dropout before it happens. To achieve this, the following activities were performed.

- Feature engineering to obtain optimal subset.
- Model building and analysis of performance.
- Hyperparameter optmization (HPO) using grid and random search methods.

2.1   Features Selection and Data Preprocessing

Researchers have provided varied definitions of school dropout, leading to inconsistencies in the literature and the use of synonymous terms. Despite the concept of dropout being straightforward, reaching a universally agreed definition has proven challenging. Moreover, students who initially drop out may later choose to return to school or continue their studies elsewhere. This perspective suggests that dropouts may not always remain dropouts permanently and should be considered as potential repeaters in different contexts [30].

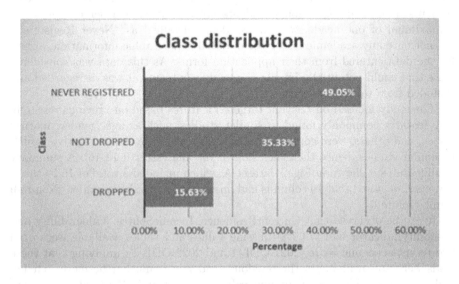

Fig. 1. Students categories based on academic records

Different scenarios can lead to students leaving school, and not all of them are classified as dropout. Examples include death or transferring to another educational institution and enrolling in a different program. LUANAR has defined various categories of school dropout based on specific circumstances surrounding the reasons for leaving. For instance, if a student departs due to death, it falls under the category of Death Withdrawal (WD), while pregnancy related departures are categorized as Pregnancy Withdrawal (PW). However, it's worth noting that certain studies conducted in other institutions may not consider these categories as school dropout, particularly in cases of death or voluntary transfers to other educational institutions [30]. This study has defined **dropout** as "scenario where a student who enroles into a program at an institution but does not finish their study cycle and graduate at that particular institution due to individual or institutional related factors."

In the case of this study, data was collected from SARIS, comprising 6,239 student records from LUANAR ODL campus between 2016 and 2021. The study focused on four out of eight programs running under ODL. The data was categorized into two groups using the students' academic semester records: 975 records were labeled as 'Dropped,' and 2,204 records were labeled as 'Not Dropped.' The classification was based on the study's definition of school dropout and LUANAR's academic rules, which allow students to reserve a place for up to one year. It was also observed that some students classified as 'Dropped' had been admitted to the institution but either did not report for studies or reported but did not register for any semester. These cases were classified as 'Never Registered'.

According to Fig. 1, the percentage of students who never reported is 49.05% of the total targeted population sample. This presents a significant withdrawal without notice issue for new students as indicated. According to LUANAR's students' rules and regulations, students are permitted to reserve a place for a maximum of one academic year. Students classified as "Never Registered" did not have any academic history or updated demographic information, except for the data entered from their application forms. As this data was considered noise that could potentially impact the study's outcome, it was disregarded and excluded from further analysis.

The study focused on relevant targeted features based on previous research. Key features commonly found in similar studies, such as age, gender, marital status, and others, were considered. These features have shown positive results in similar studies, hence their inclusion in the analysis. [10,12,16]. A summary of all features is shown in Fig. 2 dataset A, which included a total of 15 features. However, we noted that 10 columns had missing values as shown under "Non-null count" column.

It can be observed that CurrentResidence, IncomeSource, Vulnerability and DisabilityIndicator had (73.2%) missing values and values available were from two recent academic years (2021-ODL-1 and 2022-ODL-2), implying that these fields were not available in the previous academic years. Furthermore, religion had the highest number of missing values (91.3%) and ODLCentre only had about half of the total values available. The study, therefore, disregarded all

#	Column	Non-Null Count	Dtype
	RangeIndex: 3179 entries, 0 to 3178		
	Data columns (total 15 columns):		
0	WithdrawalHistory	3179 non-null	object
1	RepeatHistory	3179 non-null	object
2	MaritalStatus	2556 non-null	object
3	Gender	2918 non-null	object
4	Age	3179 non-null	int64
5	District	3092 non-null	object
6	Religion	276 non-null	object
7	StudentType	3178 non-null	object
8	ProgrammeCode	3179 non-null	object
9	employmentStatus	3179 non-null	object
10	ODLCenter	1546 non-null	object
11	DisabilityIndicator	852 non-null	object
12	Vulnerability	852 non-null	object
13	IncomeSource	852 non-null	object
14	CurrentResidence	852 non-null	object
	dtypes: int64(1), object(14)		
	Dataset A		

#	Column	Non-Null Count	Dtype
	Data columns (total 10 columns):		
0	WithdrawalHistory(WH)	3179 non-null	int64
1	RepeatHistory(RH)	3179 non-null	int64
2	MaritalStatus(MS)	3179 non-null	int64
3	Gender	3179 non-null	int64
4	Age	3179 non-null	int64
5	District	3179 non-null	int64
6	StudentType(ST)	3179 non-null	int64
7	ProgrammeCode(PC)	3179 non-null	int64
8	employmentStatus(ES)	3179 non-null	int64
9	Target	3179 non-null	int64
	dtypes: int64(10)		
	Dataset B		

Fig. 2. Feature summary of collected dataset

columns with more than 50% missing data to avoid affecting the outcome of the study. However, StudentType, District, Gender and MaritalStatus were considered for the study. The missing values in these features were replaced with zeros and we also noted that the Age column had zero values for some records which were replaced by the median age value. Additionally, the data had to conform to sci-kit learn and adopted algorithms which require numeric values. As such the data was remapped to convert all non-numerical data to numerical data. For instance, 1 represented the dropped class and 0 represented the active class. The final dataset (Dataset B), had 10 features as shown in Fig. 2.

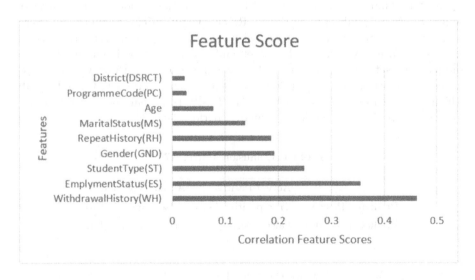

Fig. 3. Feature selection with all features

3   Analysis Based on Machine Learning

3.1   Feature Engineering

This process selects a subset of features that have high contribution to the predictable variable or class. This improves the accuracy of trained models, reduces training time due to reduced data and furthermore it reduces over-fitting. This study adopted the Filter technique and used correlation based performance evaluation criteria to rank the features [27,28]. Literature shows that Filter approaches have been used in many studies [2,10,12,16]. Additionally, they are known to utilise few resources in the feature selection process and have the ability of processing huge data sizes [29]. This study first generated a Pearson correlation heatmap using seaborn and matplotlib in order to map correlation values of all independent variables and the dependent variable (target variable). The absolute correlation values against the target variable were filtered out and features were then selected based on the correlation values. The study used a threshold of 0.2. The dataset had 9 features, however after dropping all features below the threshold, only three features remained which are WithdrawalHistory (WH), EmploymentStatus (ES) and StudentType(ST), as shown in Fig. 3. Three features were also successfully used in a study to reduce school dropout in Tanzania [10].

3.2   Experiment Procedure and Evaluation Metrics

The study adopted four supervised classification algorithms from the following domains: Bayesian, Regression, Instance based and Ensemble. These were represented by Gaussian Naïve Bayes (NB), Logistic Regression (LR), K-Nearest Neighbour (KNN)and Random Forest (RF) respectively. Three experiments were conducted: the first experiment was with the final original dataset, the second experiment used over sampled dataset and the third experiment used under sampled dataset. The performance of the classification algorithms was evaluated using four metrics. Accuracy, F-Measure, Area Under Curve (AUC) and Recall which are based on confusion matrix [17]. Lastly Hyperparameter optmization for the best performing models to enhance performance.

Table 1. Confusion Matrix [17]

	Actual Positive	Actual Negative
Predicted Positive	True positive (Tp)	False negative (Fn)
Predicted Negative	False positive (Fp)	True negative (Tn)

Based on Table 1, below are the formulas.

$$Accuracy(acc) = \frac{Tp + Tn}{Tp + Fp + Tn + Fn} \qquad (1)$$

$$Recall(r) = \frac{Tp}{Tp + Tn} \qquad (2)$$

$$F - measure(Fm) = \frac{2 * (precision * recall)}{(precision + recall)} \qquad (3)$$

$$AUC = \int (TPrate(FPrate))dFPrate \qquad (4)$$

In this study data was split into training sets (2702), Validation (477) and Testing (477). The models were trained using 70% of the data set, then used 15% to validate the performance and the remaining 15% unseen test set was used to test the performance of the models. Data splitting was aimed at exposing and checking how the model would respond to unseen data and further reduced biasness in performance results. The study adopted the stratified k-fold cross validation sampling with K = 10, this was applied to all instances of the experiment. K-fold basically exposes the algorithm to different distributions of data K-times. This further reduces bias that may occur during splitting of data into training, validation, and test sets.

3.3 Experiment 1: Model Training Using Original Dataset

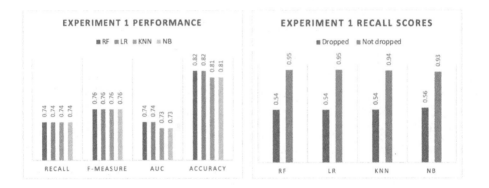

Fig. 4. Experiment 1 performance results

The aim of this experiment was to assess the performance of the models based on the original dataset of 3179 records. According to Fig. 4, RF and LR had the highest accuracy score of 82% and AUC score of 0.74. This was followed by KNN and NB all of which showed a score of 81%. Furthermore, the F-measure score for all classifiers emerged with average F-measure and Recall scores of 0.76 and 0.74 respectively. Variation in this experiment was mainly observed in Accuracy and AUC results but were minimal. However, class-based recall scores were also showing a bias towards the majority class. This is illustrated in Fig. 4, where recall scores for 'Not dropped' class is above 90% compared to scores of below

60% for the 'Dropped' class for all the models. This meant that the models were more sensitive in classifying samples in the majority class. This bias was probably due to class imbalances, the study adopted Synthetic Minority Over-sampling Technique (SMOTE) and Random Under Sampling (RUS) to handle the problem and two experiments were designed based on the oversampling and under sampling techniques.

3.4   Imbalanced Data Distribution

The problem with imbalanced data happens when observations in one class are much higher or lower than the other class such that it tends to affect the sensitivity of ML algorithms. In most cases the minority is class negligible and ends up with lower recall values. The study observed that the "Dropout" class comprised of 31% (975 samples) of the total and "Not dropped" class had 69% (2204 samples) as indicated in Fig. 5. A clear indication that the classes were not well balanced. According to literature imbalanced data tends to have effects on model performance. Therefore, to solve this problem, the study adopted SMOTE and RUS techniques to re-sample the dataset. After running SMOTE the "Dropped" class samples increased from 975 to 1880 whilst after running RUS the "Not dropped" class reduced from 2204 to 822 samples as illustrated in Fig. 5.

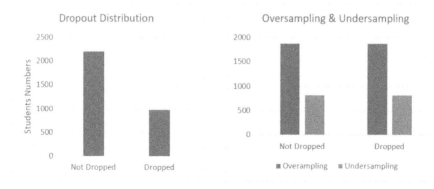

Fig. 5. Data distribution

3.5   Experiment 2: Model Training with Oversampled Dataset

The aim of this experiment was to assess the algorithms performance using the SMOTE dataset. This was considered to improve the classifiers' biasness. This experiment used a dataset of 3760 samples to build the models. However, the test set sample from the original dataset was maintained for consistency purposes. KNN had high scores in terms of averaged recall, F-measure and AUC but had the lowest accuracy score of 69%. Again, in terms of class-based recall results,

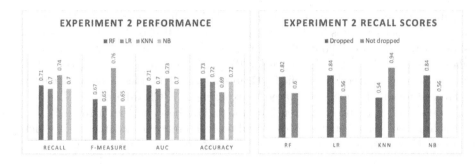

Fig. 6. Experiment 2 performance results using SMOTE dataset

KNN was still biased towards the majority class unlike the other classifiers. All evaluation criteria results dropped for all classifiers in this experiment compared to experiment 1 as shown in Fig. 6. However, RF, KNN and NB performance in terms of class-based Recall results improved with a reduced difference of about 20% between the "Dropped" and "Not dropped" class compared to around 40% difference in experiment 1. This shifted the sensitivity biasness toward the minor class. Overall RF emerged the best classifier in this experiment as observed in Fig. 6. Where RF shows a smallest gap between "Dropped" and "Not Dropped" classes. Furthermore, equal performance was observed for LR and NB.

3.6   Experiment 3: Model Training with Undersampled Dataset

The aim of this experiment was to assess the algorithms performance using RUS dataset. Again, this was considered to improve the biasness and improve the model's performance. This experiment used a dataset of 1644 samples to build the models. Similarly, to Experiment 2, the test set sample from the original dataset was maintained for consistency purposes.

Fig. 7. Experiment 3 performance results using RUS dataset

According to Fig. 7, RF and LR had the best performance. Again, accuracy results showed that RF and LR all had the highest scores of 74% which only had

1% difference compared to experiment 2 and KNN had the highest AUC score. Despite LR better scores in all evaluation criterias, LR class-based Recall scores shows a wider gap of about 30% between the "Dropped" and "Not dropped" classes compared to 18% difference for RF. Furthermore, it was observed that the number of correctly classified "Dropped" class samples also significantly increased for all classifiers compared to experiment 1. Class-based Recall scores improved with a reduced difference of about 20% between the "Dropped" and "Not dropped" class compared to around 40% difference in experiment 1, which shifted the sensitivity biasness toward the minor class as shown in Fig. 7.

3.7   Hyper-parameter Optimisation

The aim of this step is to assess predictive performance through application of HPO techniques which in other terms is a process of fine-tuning models by adjusting the models inbuilt configuration also known as hyperparameters [24–26]. According to experiment 2 and 3, RF emerged the best classifier in all experiments. In this case, we considered the best performing models under RUS and SMOTE , then random search and grid search methods were applied. The study conducted two experiments based on both random and grid approaches for each algorithm. The aim was to check how each algorithm would perform using either of the HPO techniques. Table 2 shows results of model tuning process, the table shows best scores and hyperparameters for each method. During the experiments, the study maintained the configured hyperparameters constant for each algorithm and method. The aim was to avoid biases in terms of performance between randomized and grid searches. According to these results, it was noted that there was not any significant improvement when SMOTE dataset was used, however, the study was still able to uncover the best performing Hyperparameters. On the other hand, RUS dataset showed an improvement compared to the default settings as shown in Fig. 8.

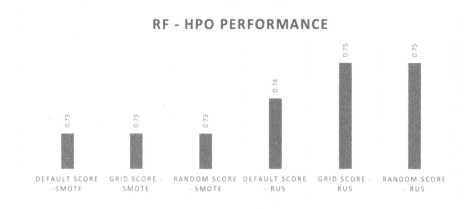

Fig. 8. HPO results comparison

Table 2. RF parameters with random and grid search methods

Search Method	Score	Best Parameters
Random	75	n_estimators: 100, min_samples_split: 2, min_samples_leaf: 6, max_depth: 8, criterion: 'gini'
Grid	75	criterion: gini; max_depth: 2, min_samples_leaf: 2, min_samples_split: 4, n_estimators: 115

4   Discussion

There have been several studies in Malawi which have looked at school dropout, however, most of them have focused on school dropout after it has already happened [3,5,6,13–15]. This study attempted to assess the feasibility of predicting school dropout using ML algorithms. Since 2016 to 2021 LUANAR had 975 dropped out students under ODL. According to [10], small numbers of dropped out students are common in school dropout problems and this was expected in this study, however, in the case of LUANAR, the number was small but if compared to other studies [11,12,16,17], 15.6% was on the higher side. This means that school dropout was a serious problem in LUANAR ODL system.

Worth noting is the variation in terms of how institutions define school dropout. This means that school dropout prediction problems also depends on how a study defines what school dropout means to be able to draw a line between active students and dropout students. [19,20,22,23].The use of ML feature engineering, enabled automation of selecting features with high impact on school dropout. The study observed that students with history of school withdrawal had high risk of dropping out of school. In a quest to determine the best classifier among the selected algorithms, the study conducted three experiments using four supervised ML classifiers from the following domains; Bayesian, Regression, Instance based, and Ensemble. This was to widen the catch unlike focusing on one domain.

The problem of class imbalance is common in school dropout problems since in most cases the number of students who dropout of school is usually lower compared to number of active students for many institutions [10]. RF using undersampling and oversampling solved the problem by reducing the biasness between "Dropped" and "Not dropped" classes. Again, RF with undersampling proved to improve performance when exposed to HPO using both random and grid search methods compared to model default settings. Furthermore, it was noted that there is no standardized formula for setting hyperparameters. Researchers manually set hyperparameters, unlike parameters that are automatically configured during the model learning process based on the training dataset. Consequently, there may be unexplored options in this study regarding HPO, as indicated by available literature [24,25]. Again, limited processing power constrained certain parameter range values to control processing.

5   Conclusion

A space in public university is a golden opportunity for the learner and the country's economy particularly so in developing countries like Malawi. Completion of higher education entails better employment opportunity, sound labour force and higher confidence levels in their carrier and country at large. However, school dropout is posing as a challenge in developing countries. Precise prediction of who will dropout and why they will dropout remains a challenge for higher education managers in developing countries. This also limits sound interventions to safeguard dropouts or to avoid avoidable dropouts. This research was therefore designed to fill the knowledge gap and provide tools for predicting school dropout using machine learning models run on data obtained from a Learning Management Systems. This work has refined and provided easy to use model for forecasting school dropout in Malawi.

References

1. Alice, K., Folorunso, O., Lateef, U.: Predicting students' grade scores using training functions of artificial neural network. J. Nat. Sci. Eng. Technol. **14**(February), 25–42 (2015)
2. Aulck, L., Velagapudi, N., Blumenstock, J., West, J.: Predicting Student Dropout in Higher Education (2016). http://arxiv.org/abs/1606.06364
3. Brossard, M., Diane, C., Michael, M.: The Education System in Malawi (2010). https://doi.org/10.1596/978-0-8213-8198-4
4. Chawinga, W.D., Zozie, P.A.: Increasing access to higher education through open and distance learning: empirical findings from Mzuzu University, Malawi. Int. Rev. Res. Open Distance Learn. **17**(4), 1–20 (2016). https://doi.org/10.19173/irrodl. v17i4.2409
5. Chibambo, M., Wellman, K.: Are peerless e-resources any better tools for supporting students in open and distance learning environments than the more traditional tools? The case of Mzuzu University, Malawi. Res. World: J. Arts Sci. Commerce **VIII**(3), 126–138 (2017). https://doi.org/10.18843/rwjasc/v8i3/14
6. Janerose, Y.: School Feeding Programmes in Chimutu, Malawi: Opportunities, benefits and challenges. University of Fort Hare (2013). http://hdl.handle.net/20. 500.11837/522
7. Lee, S., Chung, J.Y.: The machine learning-based dropout early warning system for improving the performance of dropout prediction. Appl. Sci. (Switzerland) **9**(15) (2019). https://doi.org/10.3390/app9153093
8. Lottering, R., Hans, R., Lall, M.: A machine learning approach to identifying students at risk of dropout: a case study. Int. J. Adv. Comput. Sci. Appl. **11**(10). https://doi.org/10.14569/ijacsa.2020.0111052
9. Ministry of Education: 2019 Malawi Education Statistics Report (2019)
10. Mduma, N., Kalegele, K., Machuve, D.: A survey of machine learning approaches and techniques for student dropout prediction. Data Sci. J. **18**(1) (2019). https:// doi.org/10.5334/dsj-2019-014

11. Mduma, N., Kalegele, K., Machuve, D.: Machine learning approach for reducing student's dropout rates. Int. J. Adv. Comput. Res. **9**(42), 156–169 (2019). https://doi.org/10.19101/ijacr.2018.839045
12. Mgala, M.: Investigating Prediction Modelling of Academic Performance for Students in Rural Schools in Kenya. University of Cape Town (2016). http://hdl.handle.net/11427/23463
13. Mzuza, M.K., Yudong, Y., Kapute, F.: Analysis of factors causing poor passing rates and high dropout rates among primary school girls in Malawi. World J. Educ. **4**(1) (2014). https://doi.org/10.5430/wje.v4n1p48
14. Naunje, C.W.: ScholarWorks@UMass Amherst The Magnitude and Causes of Dropout in Malawi: A Study of Chiradzulu District (2014). https://scholarworks.umass.edu/cie_capstones/47
15. Pike, I., Grant, M.: Gifting Relationships and School Dropout in Rural Malawi: Examining Differences by Gender and Poverty Level (2019)
16. Ramphele, F.: Predicting grade progression within the Limpopo Education System. University of Cape Town (2018). http://hdl.handle.net/11427/30137
17. Stapel, M., Zheng, Z., Pinkwart, N.: An ensemble method to predict student performance in an online math learning environment. In: Proceedings of the 9th International Conference on Educational Data Mining. EregulDM 2016, pp. 231–238 (2016)
18. Umar, F., Ussiph, N.: Appraisal of the classification technique in data mining of student performance using j48 decision tree, K-nearest neighbor and multilayer perceptron algorithms. Int. J. Comput. Appl. **179**(33), 39–46 (2018). https://doi.org/10.5120/ijca2018916751
19. Adam, S., Adom, D., Bediako, A.B.: The Major Factors That Influence Basic School Dropout in Rural Ghana: The Case of Asunafo South District in the Brong Ahafo Region of Ghana, vol. 7, no. 28. (2016). www.iiste.org
20. Gudeta O.: Factors Affecting Students' Dropout in Secondary Schools of Wayu Tuka Woreda East Wollega Zone Oromya Regional State Department of Educational Planning and Management: College of Education and Behavioral Studies, Addis Ababa University Addis Ababa Ethiopia (2019)
21. Hurwitz, J., Kirsch, D.: Machine Learning IBM Limited Edition (2018). http://www.wiley.com/go/permissions
22. Kavetuna, J.: Formal Education Open Schooling (n.d.)
23. Mahoney, J.L.: School dropout. In: Bornstein, M.H. (ed.) The SAGE Encyclopedia of Lifespan Human Development, pp. 1889–1891. SAGE, Thousand Oaks (2018). https://www.researchgate.net/publication/326098844
24. Mantovani, R.G., Rossi, A.L.D., Alcobaça, E., Gertrudes, J.C., Junior, S.B., de Carvalho, A.C.P.D.L.F.: Rethinking default values: a low cost and efficient strategy to define hyperparameters. arXiv preprint arXiv:2008.00025 (2020)
25. Matache, C., Passerat, J., Kainz, B.: Efficient Design of Machine Learning Hyperparameter Optimizers. MEng Individual Project, pp. 17–18. Imperial College London (2019)
26. Tran, N., Schneider, J.G., Weber, I., Qin, A.K.: Hyper-parameter optimization in classification: to-do or not-to-do. Pattern Recogn. **103**, 107245 (2020). https://doi.org/10.1016/j.patcog.2020.107245
27. Kumar, V.: Feature selection: a literature review. Smart Comput. Rev. **4** (2014). https://doi.org/10.6029/smartcr.2014.03.007
28. Kumar, G., Kumar, K.: An information theoretic approach for feature selection. Secur. Commun. Netw. **5**, 178–185 (2012). https://doi.org/10.1002/sec.303

29. BolónCanedo, V., Remeseiro, B., Cancela, B.: Feature Selection for Big Visual Data: Overview and Challenges (2018). https://doi.org/10.1007/978-3-319-93000-8_16

30. Yokozeki, Y.: The causes, processes and consequences of student drop-out from Junior Secondary School (JSS) in Ghana: the case of Komenda-Edina-Eguafo-Abrem (K.E.E.A.) district (1996)

Co-creation Lab and Its Liminal Pedagogy as an Innovation Tool for Shaping a Local and Global Future

Delma Rodriguez Morales[✉]

Pre-doctoral Fellow at the International University of La Rioja, La Rioja, Logroño, Spain
anillacultural.directora@gmail.com

Abstract. The article presents the co-creative process carried out in a distributed laboratory on the Internet, crossing continents and different cultures to generate something new in networking. From a transdisciplinary approach of art, science, technology and society, the outcomes, lessons learned and main prospective features for further research and intervention of the project in e-learning, e-culture, multilingual platform, etc. are evidenced. The text covers the first edition of the Co-creation Lab 2019 and its process to date.

Keywords: co-creation · innovation · e-learning · e-culture · multilingual tools · art and science · NRENs

1 Background Information

Anilla Cultural (Cultural Ring), born in 2007–08 in Catalonia and expanded from 2010 to Latin America (http://anillacultural.net/), is a network of co-creation and collaboration in art, science, technology and society through advanced Internet, conceived as such in its founding the technological infrastructure as it mainly worked through telecommunications systems. For instance, H323, known as packed-based multimedia communications systems for point-to-point and multi-point conferences (https://www.itu.int/rec/T-REC-H.323-202203-I/en), required a robust Internet at that time (known as advanced Internet) and specific equipment for transmissions. Until 2019, this technological deployment continued to function. While at the same time other forms of video conferencing in web environments were gaining ground in terms of the number of users and platforms available.

Currently, the Uruguay Cultural Ring (or Anilla Cultural) and its global networks interoperate on all types of systems and platforms, depending on the type of activity, project or proposal to be developed. For instance, certain specialised tools are used for interactive and distributed concerts, while other types of platforms are used for interactive mass videoconferences, and these types of scenarios can be combined.

D. Rodriguez Morales—Director, Cultural Ring UY & its global networks.

D. Crawford et al. (Eds.): TIE 2023, LNICST 575, pp. 17–36, 2024.
https://doi.org/10.1007/978-3-031-59383-3_2

The founding objective of the Anilla Cultural was to facilitate access to quality cultural content with global, regional and local references of new media art and to encourage the co-creation of different audiences for a contemporary cultural transformation.

The Anilla Cultural node in Uruguay arose from an invitation to participate from the founding nodes in Ibero-America (https://anillaculturaluruguay.net/), initiating actions in November 2011 (https://rb.gy/anyyc), and from the beginning it had its own profile, contextualised to the reality of Uruguay inserted in a regional and global level. Therefore, maintaining the characteristics of a network of co-creation in art, science, technology and society through the Internet, a decentralised proposal was designed, distributed in all the country, (https://anillaculturaluruguay.net/quienes-somos/) not restricted to an only institution and at the same time integrating several multi-stakeholders. The people from all the provinces in Uruguay have been participating in more than 10 years of trajectory, and also the Uruguayan node has a very active role leading activities for the Iberoamerican region on a global and local level.

In the 2017–18 time period, the Anilla Cultural Uruguay visualised the need to deepen lines of action in the founding bases such as co-creation, the conference "Co-creators over Internet" synthesises this vision (https://vimeo.com/282518942) and establishes the main keys on which projects will be developed in the coming years.

For this reason, in this context the Co-creation Lab (https://anillaculturaluruguay.net/lab-co-creacion-postulacion-a-co-creadores/) was announced in March 2019.

1.1 Co-creation Lab: An Intervention and Research Initiative

The Co-Creation Lab is a research and intervention project in the aforementioned framework. The proposal is a transdisciplinary approach in arts and science mediated by ICT to network collective creation through the advanced Internet. The Laboratory (Lab) for human and technological experimentation will have a distributed modality where the participants or potential co-creators will be in live connection from different countries, regions and continents.

There are two ways to access the co-creator role: a global call with selection or an invitation letter; this last option was not developed in the first edition.

The first edition of the Lab, held in 2019, was open to everyone over the age of eighteen who is studying and/or working in the fields of arts, science, technology and society, such as artists, scientists, engineers, technicians, designers, teachers, makers, etc. (https://anillaculturaluruguay.net/lab-co-creacion-postulacion-a-co-creadores/).

The age population was very heterogeneous in the call from eighteen to sixty-five years of age and remained so until the last stages of the project.

There was an open call process,-it was disseminated all over the world, focusing on people to manage one language as Spanish, or English, or Portuguese-, that involved some steps to be completed. Such as: sending the registration form with their data, sending their biography, a letter of intent or interest in why they were applying and then those who completed these stages signed a work agreement, regarding the confidentiality of information, agreeing to participate in a research project, free tuition, etc. Among other specific characteristics, such as that the participant and potential co-creator could leave the Lab whenever they wanted, but could not return again, etc.

Throughout the process of interacting with potential co-creators, a mutually beneficial atmosphere was clearly presented, especially the benefits of becoming a co-creator through the Lab. Along with this, the Lab offered: training the areas proposed, ICT tools for multilingual interlinking and for group and individual interventions, different types of international referents (such as, Claudio Allocchio, Justin Trieger, Tom Gorman, Bryan Rill and Matti Hämäläinen, Domenico Vicinanza, among others), advisers and technicians to assist groups in their co-creations, and local and global networking and dissemination actions for co-creators and their final productions. In summary, the Lab offered in the first edition, two overview guidelines of: "I) Multicultural learning processes in the generation of new ideas - projects, etc., and II) ICT mediation skills in a fruitful environment of exchange". (https://rb.gy/e472h).

Another feature in the Lab's distributed collaboration is that NRENs, known by their acronym for National Research and Education Networks https://about.geant.org/nrens/-, constituted part of technological solutions for research development.

In this way, a transnational group of education, research and academic networks in Uruguay (RAU), Mexico (CUDI), Colombia (RENATA), Ecuador (CEDIA), Brazil (RNP), of the Latin American region (*Red* CLARA), in the United States (Internet 2) and Europe (GARR and GÉANT) offered human and technological support in different areas and moments of the project.

1.2   e-Culture as a Setting for the Co-creation Lab

The e-Culture as a field in permanent growth and conceptual conformation, contains two main perspectives. One of them is related to the idea of connectedness to the preservation of cultural heritage, with a certain counterpoint to commercial or business aspects (Ronchi, 2009) interrelated to other areas such as e-Government, e-Services, etc., with the "human factor" and the strategy of co-creation as crucial elements in this multi-stakeholder interweaving of e-culture (Ronchi, 2022). And another international referent of the field states that the e-Culture is associated with interdisciplinary studies between artists and scientists, among others, who create various digital manifestations on Internet networks and related devices (Baeva, 2017). Baeva extends these two natures of e-Culture by expressing the need to establish a "third nature" (Baeva, 2019, p. 513), focusing on creative interactions and technological mediation. In this sense, Baeva positions a step forward to be built in the field of e-Culture, related to the "systematisation of electronic culture" (Baeva, 2018, p. 328). In this line, the relevance of the contribution that this article and others already documented as an outcome of the intervention and research projects of Anilla Cultural Uruguay and its global networks is focused (Rodriguez Morales, 2020).

In particular, co-creation can enable the design of cyber-technologies that keep people at the centre, in conjunction with the humanities and digital humanities, in this area of e-Culture. Thus, co-creation, understood in its etymological root by the Latin root prefix co-, *cum*, meaning with, together with creation, implying the production of something new or of value for mutual benefit or for the benefit of the parties concerned (Rill and Hämäläinen, 2018). It is linked in practice to a field understood as art, which is why co-creation cannot be engineered.

From this perspective of co-creation as art, Rill and Hämäläinen (2018) argue that "co-creation is for everyone" (p. 6), mainly related to transdisciplinary practices (p. 56) and linked to cooperation, collaboration and collective intelligence, with its own nature in how to organise multiple techniques, ideas and motivations that can be effectively converged.

In essence, "co-creating is a meta-level process that harnesses the creative potential of all groups, enhancing collective creativity and driving innovation and cultural change" (Rill and Hämäläinen, 2018, p.12).

2   Multiple Deployments with the Newcomers

This section presents the multiple deployments that took place with newcomers to co-create or potential co-creators, who completed the proposed process in the laboratory and were awarded a co-creator certificate in art, science, technology and society.

Here, then, actions that were designed and finally carried out are compiled, together with information on the interaction of the participants.

After the global call for applications to participate in the Lab, eighty-seven applications were collected from four continents (Americas, Europe, Africa and Oceania), of which forty applications were left to start in the Lab. The selection of participants was based on the criteria that all those who applied the form of the requirements and completed the biography requests (to know their expertise and training) and signed the memorandum of understanding accepting to be part of the target population of the research. Along with a confidentiality agreement on the information of the co-creation process, among others, were admitted.

At the end of the process, it was agreed that the productions and their co-creators would be made public, but during the process intangibles were protected. Therefore, the information was to be restricted to the participants. Also on the part of the laboratory, the anonymity of the participants associated with the process was preserved, and only the findings were to be used for the purposes of the scientific study. Another important aspect was that the applicants knew that they had to comply with three compulsory online meetings and other actions proposed as part of the agenda of activities. Also, together with the estimated weekly time they would need to participate in the laboratory, in addition to knowing the work methodology.

Therefore, prior to the launch of the Lab, participants were very clear about the scope of involvement that the Lab would demand of them for four months (May to September) in 2019.

A significant degree of expectation was also maintained about details that did not need to be disclosed and did not alter the signed agreements. But concerned specific actions that were designed to generate curiosity and motivation among participants.

The agreements of understanding offered guarantees to those who had a genuine interest in participating and experiencing co-creation. Also, this was the criterion of transparency in the selection of participants, i.e. all those who wanted to and completed (on time) the formalities could have access to participate.

The main stages were the formation of groups, facilitation of ICT tools, virtual meeting points (synchronous and asynchronous), generation of prototypes by the co-creative groups, rehearsals or testing actions and practices or staging.

The thematic profile of the Lab was in arts and science and technology, focusing on performing arts through the Internet. Figure 1, depicts these stages, which were previously conceived in the design of the Lab, and were adapted to the requirements of the co-creative groups as they developed.

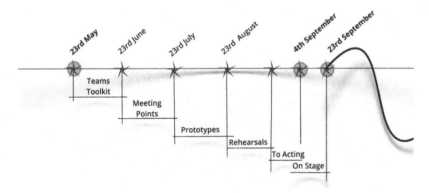

Fig. 1. Agenda of the four-month Lab and its planned stages of implementation.

The launch of the laboratory (23rd May 2019) coincided with the first hybrid meeting (online and face-to-face for those who were in the city of Montevideo), held in the Auditorium of the Faculty of Engineering of the UdelaR. The participants were given a digital dossier of all the potential co-creators as a form of initial interrelationship, detailing the areas of each one, their skills and interests for co-creation. This type of material was like unveiling the unknown and expectation of who they were and was activated as a letter of introduction of each one to the others.

At the same event, the participants were given lectures by the aforementioned experts on the topics of co-creation in advanced Internet networks in art, science and technology (in this playlist you can find the recordings of the lectures: https://cutt.ly/CwqGrO44). In real time, within the Pexip video conference platform (https://www.pexip.com/) there were audio channels with simultaneous interpretation into Spanish, Portuguese and English, thus covering the languages of origin of all participants. The format of this videoconference interoperates between several systems at the same time. From H323 rooms where the interpreters of each language were located, the conference room with participants in Montevideo (H323 and via web) and the different connections via web of the speakers and participants distributed in the four continents. Also at this event, each participant was provided with a virtual toolkit (CISCO Webex meetings, CISCO Webex Teams, Zoom, Pexip, etc.) for synchronous and asynchronous work. For instance, in the asynchronous communication spaces the participants would write (in his/her language) a message for the group and by adding the bot tools, the same message would be displayed in Spanish, English and Portuguese. This type of experience was fundamental for the period after the first synchronous general workshop meetings, where it allowed for continuity and reinforced the idea of interconnection and communication without borders.

This type of deployment, and others mentioned in the article, was possible thanks to the collaboration of national and regional academic networks of education and research (NRENs).

Figure 2, is shown the map of the Co-creation Lab, containing the geographical reference of the participants and of those who supported or formed the proposal as a team.

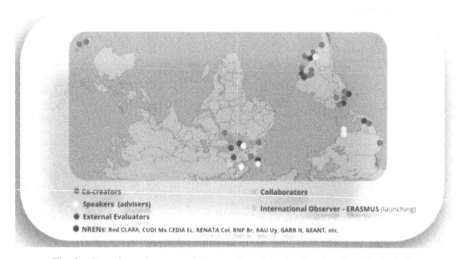

Fig. 2. Georeferencing map of the people and institutions involved in the Lab.

The organisational chart of the Lab, then, was made up of the potential co-creators as the core or target population. And around them were the roles of collaborators (such as technical facilitators and advisers of the co-creation process), the speakers of the initial event also in the development had advisory roles. Both for the co-creative groups and for the interventions and research of the Lab. There were also the groups of interpreters who were there throughout the four-month process, both for the formative meetings and for specific synchronous meetings of the co-creative groups. And there was another group of consultants who,- although this possibility had been designed beforehand-, from the Lab waited to visualise the type of consultant required according to the needs of the co-creative groups. In other words, the role was outlined without first identifying the type of expert to be consulted, waiting for the co-creative groups to define their proposals. This was only visualised in (the second part of) the middle of the laboratory process and they were called in as soon as the groups needed support within the profile of art, science, technology and society.

To aid the Lab's transnational team, there were several members of the NRENs who coordinated their technical teams together with the Lab's coordination. Figure 3 illustrates the organisation chart of roles, which indicates the position described below in the functioning of the laboratory.

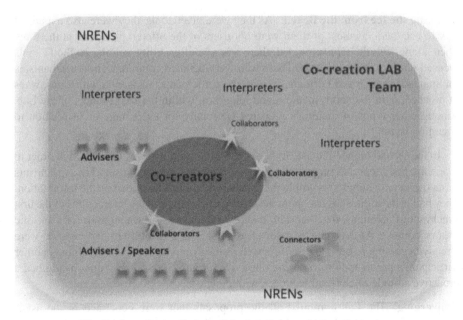

Fig. 3. Organisational chart of the Lab Team and its participants.

2.1 Playing and Learning How to Play the Game

From the perspective of Rill and Hämäläinen (2018), the process is defined as the "co-creation journey" because of the non-linear aspects involved.

In the first and second month of the laboratory and after the launch event, an activity called "brains on the beach" was planned, which is part of the aforementioned book and aims for potential co-creators to exchange ideas and interests in order to facilitate co-creation. In that event, the proposal was made in the same sense, although the role it played was more one of socialisation rather than initiating the exchange of ideas for co-creation. In any case, the synchronous meetings (some were held via Zoom with simultaneous interpretation if required and others via CISCO Webex Meetings for video conferencing) of "brains on the beach", where synchronous virtual spaces (virtual background, and also beach clothing, etc.) were set up. For instance, as if they were on the beach and the Lab team dressed according to a Caribbean environment to reinforce the idea of being in a relaxed, comfortable and playful attitude of interaction. This last aspect was well received by most of the synchronous participants who showed themselves in their natural domestic environment (studio, home, office, etc.) in front of the other participants who were just starting to get to know and interact with each other. They even synchronously shared their pets live, as a positive form of rapprochement, or accompanied them with appropriate clothing according to the beach concept, etc. After these meetings, in the asynchronous exchange spaces in the virtual classroom of CISCO Webex Teams, which allows the use of language bots. The interaction with incipient ideas, proposals or simply something to share began to be visualised more intensively.

Breaking the Ice from the Beach. As they were given tools, they were also explained how to use them, as most of them were not users of the offered platforms at the time. Then, along with the tools provided, there was a brief usability training on the IT tools focused on the Lab's proposals. There were very detailed communication mechanisms (in Spanish, English and Portuguese) with the participants, an agenda with dates, ways of proceeding in the short, medium and long term within the four months of the Lab. Among other types of materials prepared especially for each stage or in relation to emerging issues.

In the second month, the use of the synchronous platform was intensified in order to shape the first ideas and proposals put forward in the initial exercises. The participants formed groups or subgroups within the asynchronous platform based on the information. They had in the digital dossier about the other participants and the interactions of the first synchronous meetings, together with their own initiative to form a group for a specific idea or purpose. At that time, profiles of leadership or continuity in participation were already beginning to be visualised. As well as the synergies involved in joining another participant's group and/or proposing one's own group. Both of these options implied a proactive attitude of constant feedback with others.

Converging. The Lab compiled all the proposals that were generated in the asynchronous classroom and in the "Meeting Points" (synchronous), the compilation was presented to all the participants to verify and give their opinion on the inclusion of other new ideas. As a result of this process, eleven ideas or proposals were generated for further work, some of which contained a wide range of articulations between art, science, technology and society. For instance, the co-creation of an interactive virtual reality video game based on the game of Hopscotch with a strong impact on citizen awareness on issues such as violence, climate change, etc. Another proposal was based on the art of scientific poly-location with the use of holograms. Also several proposals related telematic performing arts with scientific contents and other ideas linked genomic editing and quantum physics, among other possible ideas were provided from the participants.

The final compendium of the eleven ideas served to communicate to all the participants that this initial production determined the subsequent work of forming groups to continue elaborating or transforming these productions. The participants received from the Lab a document with a description of each idea, including the description of the members and the challenges they faced in the future. Also adding an indication of whether the group that had formed the idea would accept new members or not. For all these characteristics and with the goal to put a step forward, all potential co-creators were asked to confirm their participation in the second stage of the laboratory, aimed at developing prototypes. This mechanism served to define the participants and their destinations in the following groups.

From the initial number of forty participants, twenty-two people confirmed their participation in the second stage and from that moment on, working groups were formed (using the same platforms already used) to receive advice in the different stages of co-creation. The participants who confirmed to continue in the Lab stages were sent a communication as guidelines on the next steps, actions and productions of the second part and final stage.

Fertile Atmosphere for Co-creation. A different process then began for each group. One of the aspects that emerged from the natural purging of participants and proposals was that five major projects remained out of the eleven ideas proposed. This allowed for a reorganisation of the co-creation groups, along with a greater focus of purpose. Thus, the groups began to ask the Lab for help or advice on issues related to their projects. The Lab proposed possibilities for them to develop and at the same time the groups were told to direct the actions with the aim of making a presentation as a product at the final meeting on 23rd September 2019.

On the one hand, the groups were in an effervescent state, because they had found a joint work to co-create and they were also at a crossroads of tasks to solve, where some of them knew how to do them and others didn't.

On the other hand, there was a sense of motivation in the groups that were in the middle and final stage of the process. In addition, there was a sense of motivation in the groups that they were in the middle and final stage of the process. The second hybrid meeting (4th September 2019) served to strengthen and adjust all these challenges. And to interact more deeply between the potential co-creators (who were already beginning to perceive themselves as such) and their groups.

In addition, the teams started to prepare the presentation of the final meeting, in fact in this second meeting the participants defined three final projects instead of the five they had selected when they started the second stage. Within this work process, there was another process of purging in the number of participants, from twenty-two to eleven who participated in the final presentation (23rd September) of the proposed co-creation projects. Table 1, depicts the evolution of the number of applications received from four continents. The number of potential co-creators at the beginning of the intervention, the number of participants in the second stage of the project and how many reached the end of the process to become co-creators.

The reasons for these drop-outs were part of a natural process, in the very challenges of co-creation based primarily on the ability or not to converge and agree so that co-creation can flow in the process. Other declinations from participants were also due to personal circumstances beyond the laboratory's control, such as themselves expressing regret at having to leave the proposal.

Table 1. Number of Lab participants, from applications to end of project

Applications	Launching	2nd Part (Prototypes & further)	Final
87	40	22	11

At the same time, there were interesting interactions between the participants during this period, where the Lab advised them on specific co-creation counselling, while they were accompanied by other advisors on the themes of the project. This made it possible to unblock rigid group dynamics and enable them to move forward in their processes.

The second synchronous meeting of the co-creation groups (held on 4th September 2019) articulated the "Rehearsal" actions for the "Staging" with the final meeting on 23rd September 2019, where the co-creation productions were presented.

The last (hybrid) production presentation meeting was where the co-creators publicly shared their co-creation through the Pitch format. It was broadcast publicly via the Internet (in three interpretation channels: Spanish, English and Portuguese) interconnecting several communication systems on the Pexip platform. In this last meeting of the Lab, it is important to mention that the host for the event and the presence of some co-creators and the Lab team was "The Internet House of Latin America and the Caribbean" (https://www.lacnic.net/casadeInternet), which is the main hub of Internet entities in the region and is based in Montevideo. Other co-creators, the Lab's distributed team (technicians and interpreters), special guests such as Lab advisors and the jury or external evaluators invited for their expertise in each project's field were also connected.

The latter carried out an evaluation process of the three projects, which they studied in depth beforehand and gave live feedback and exchange to the co-creators. This feedback was not broadcast publicly, but was discussed exclusively with the co-creators in hybrid mode.

From this point onwards in the article and also as part of the process, those who reached the final stage are referred to as co-creators, until now they were participants, or potential co-creators. Therefore, from a symbolic point of view, having reached this stage places them in a different role, and the laboratory itself was responsible for disseminating their profiles, as this was part of the working agreement.

The Fruits of Co-creation. To summarise, the three co-created projects are called "*Rayuela*" (Hopscotch), "Performing Arts" and "Art Connections Ethology". The following is a synthesis of each one, in order to exemplify the derivations from the eleven ideas to these final proposals.

"Hopscotch" is a conceptual proposal for an interactive game in immersive virtual reality, multimedia and networked, with the aim of promoting values around caring for the planet and the beings that inhabit it. The proposal encompasses the areas of art, science, technology and society, with the aim that its location could be in a museum. The members of this group are in Uruguay and received specialised advice from designers and developers in the area and also in co-creation issues.

The co-creation group in "Performing Arts", whose members are based in Ecuador, Brazil, New Zealand, and Uruguay, offers a live telematic dance distributed in different places in Latin America and New Zealand, to represent the interconnection of living beings on the planet. Sharing microscopic images and sounds of lightning and electricity discharges, so that the spectators can have a myriad of sensations and perceptions about the proposed themes. This group made an interrelation of the formative skills of its members and also received support in areas to expand the proposal, as well as in specific aspects of co-creation.

"Art Connections Ethology" (integrated from New Zealand and Uruguay members) is a co-creation group that, based on a problem about the modification of a natural environment. They propose a series of networked encounters to raise awareness among the audience through a sensitive experience in telematic performing arts about the need to build a sustainable planet. For instance, they will address issues such as the problems of migratory birds whose flight is disorientated by high-voltage cables that alter the birds' perception of their georeferencing. Leaving the spectator with the question of how each one of us can contribute to the sustainability of the planet. This group worked with a general idea co-created, to which the members contributed in different ways, as well as receiving specialised support from experts in telematic performing arts and co-creation. (https://cutt.ly/ywqGrIFH).

After an analytical description of the actions carried out by the Lab on the main behaviours of the participants, Fig. 4, visually summarises the technological mediation processes.

In the following section, an analysis of the information collected during the four months of intervention is carried out, which is cross-referenced with the interviews conducted with the co-creators, i.e. the eleven participants who reached the end of the process. In this way, it was contrasted with the information gathered during the process and cases and situations were compared. This is how, a compendium of the lessons learned in the process itself is established, connections are made with some theoretical concepts of co-creation and a list of characteristics is made to guide good practices in co-creation.

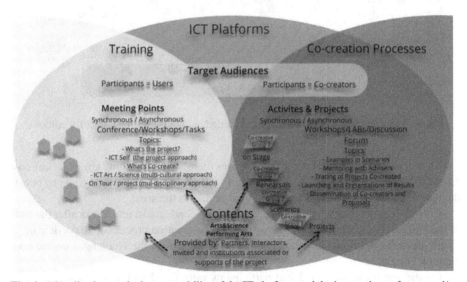

Fig. 4. Visualisation on the interoperability of the IT platform and the interactions of users and/or co-creators within the target population, the co-creation processes and their corresponding training.

3 Boosting to the Co-creators Practitioners

The participants who reached the final stage of the laboratory had in some way a form of rite of passage, in a practical and symbolic sense as considered from Cultural Anthropology (Harris, 1998). But in this case in the co-creation and its legitimation in the role of co-creator in a public way. This is evident from the interviews conducted, where they all agreed that the laboratory has been a before and after in their lives. Both personally and professionally, either because it has been positive or because it has far exceeded their previous expectations. The process of the laboratory is shown as a visual synthesis in Fig. 5, in relation to its first edition 2019.

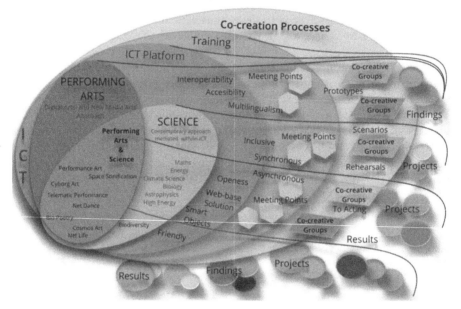

Fig. 5. Visual synthesis of the development carried out in Co-creation Lab, 2019 edition.

Therefore, this section of the article focuses on highlighting some key points of co-creation, which emerged in the process itself and which can serve as a guide to boost the role of co-creators towards a professional profile in the area.

Considering the interviews with the co-creators (conducted a few weeks after the end of the lab) and comparing with the records of the co-creation process of all participants. There are three main blocks or stages that were evident in the challenges on the co-creation practice.

On the one hand, we found that participants were faced with defining the "what", in the period of the first stage of the Lab, with the instances of the toolkit and meeting points.

On the other hand, the challenge of "how" appeared in the second stage of the Lab, from the "Meeting Points" to the final closing presentation. And finally, at the end of the four months of the laboratory, specifically the co-creators (with the certificate received from the Lab), coincidentally expressed a natural question about how to "follow up" to develop their projects.

It is noteworthy that the co-creators said that the meeting points acted as hinges, after the start, and were the link in the process of the first five projects and the three finalist projects.

In turn, the meeting points, due to their diversity of formats and contents, served as a link to the classrooms and asynchronous virtual spaces where the co-creators interacted. The content of the asynchronous spaces served as a topic for dialogue and discussion among the participants to find out what to decide in the future or to generate agreements among them.

An important characteristic that the co-creators remarked about the meeting points is that it allowed them to see (linked to hearing) and empathise or tune in with others. This aspect was mostly expressed by the co-creators. Therefore, the meeting points can be synthesised as vehicles for "empathic visualisation" (concept coined from the co-creators interviewed and the analysis of the whole co-creative process) among the future co-creators, which is a key nucleus for establishing solid interpersonal links through which communication would flow in order to co-create.

Focusing on technological mediation, from a more general point of view and not only from the co-creators' approach, we found that participants perceived an enriched environment of ICT tools to be explored. These ICT tools were positively perceived as an interweaving between the role of the Lab facilitators (multilingual bots, interpreters, Lab team, etc.) and the participants. At the same time, this environment cushioned participants from the difficulties of communication between potential co-creators. This was evident in the passage between the first and second stage, where the participants were asked who confirmed their participation in the second stage, as it required the eleven compiled ideas to be refined. Between those who decided not to continue and those who confirmed their participation, there was a clear fifty-fifty balance of attrition and permanence in the Lab.

In the second phase of the Lab, ICT tools were used for technological mediation, mainly for analysis, compilation and definition. Thus, the process of technological mediation is perceived by the co-creators as a meta-level challenge that enables them to focus specifically on their interests, motivations and inspiring ideas for co-creation. At least to analyse which of the ideas put forward by others have the greatest potential for development.

Looking beyond the participants of the Lab and focusing on its infrastructure. It must be kept in mind that the context of technological mediation provided to the participants corresponds to a complex technological and human ecosystem offered by the NRENs involved in the Lab, which have a strong track record of collaboration in this type of project. Therefore, the involvement of a transcontinental cluster of NRENs to support this type of laboratory was a key factor.

While the Lab has recorded and archived tons of videos of the different stages of the process and the interactions of its participants, very few of these videos are part of a public archive. Only very few of these videos constitute a public archive; those that have been selected as open content are intended as a strategy for disseminating co-creation in these contexts and for others to access. (https://cutt.ly/CwqGrO44).

The focus on open contents that the Lab provides is on legitimising and disseminating co-creation and its co-creators. This is an implicit characteristic of such projects that are developed in Internet communities around academic networks.

3.1 Building the Co-creation House

This section is a compendium of features to be taken into account when designing spaces that promote networked co-creation, distributed over the Internet, multilingually and interculturally. It is intended as a complement to the guide by Rill and Hämäläinen (2018), as their experiences were not developed in this modality described. And on the other hand, it aims to scientifically document an experience initiated in 2019 (prior to the pandemic, without knowing that this would happen) when there were very few or almost no similar experiences with the characteristics of this laboratory.

The following is a list of characteristics that can be used to build "The House of Co-creation", as this list has been called in the Lab's research, not as a normative instruction to be followed but as liminal considerations to make authentic co-creation flow. These characteristics found in the analysis are not subordinate to each other or detrimental to some over others, they are all necessary in the co-creation ecosystem. For instance, it is important to bear in mind that although co-creation is for everyone, there will be a natural purge in open calls as described above, so that it can develop properly and not be an inclusion or exclusion. Therefore it is necessary to consider the free association of participants as a basis and to give them very clear steps to follow in the co-creation process. It makes sense, then, that close challenges are set as a way to achieve further results. It is also important that potential co-creators perceive within the Lab that there are no external obstacles to them.

For all the technological mediation mentioned above, there needs to be an enriched environment of ICT tools together with usability design for the specific context of co-creation. In turn, the role of multiple advisors is perceived as a great facilitator and inspirer for co-creators. In the Lab's co-creation process, direct and indirect strategies need to be implemented with potential co-creators, which they can learn and implement themselves in order to create bottom-up synergies, rather than receiving top-down instructions.

In the process it is necessary to establish a permanent feedback between all parties involved, even as part of the process to include new support, if necessary. In this sense, it is necessary to promote with the participants an "expanded environment to express the self". Integrating all their profiles and variables such as time differences, the place where they live, their personalities and their own body as expression and interaction. Specifically for the co-creators two aspects are relevant: the togetherness and the otherness to converge in a common purpose. According to the co-creators, the Lab's work on these aspects will enable "the findings together" with the co-creators. In relation to this, it was relevant that "the pieces of advice for the groups", such as "the bond", "the common convergence", "the solidarity", among others, can be crucial. This advice should not be perceived by the co-creators in a top down sense, but as part of the co-creative experience of the laboratory environment.

Last but not least, in this set of characteristics is that the Lab can generate a series of strategies with the co-creators to balance the frustrations they may experience in the process. The main features of co-creation in this area have been described. And the following text develops the journey of the Lab through the pandemic period and beyond, and its redesign to incorporate the lessons learned and to anticipate other challenges.

3.2   Lines of Study Ongoing

From a macro perspective on the Lab process, we found that in addition to providing tools and facilitating processes for the participants. The Lab also explored the pedagogy of co-creation locally and globally through the Internet.

This area of study (to be explored in more depth) arose during the research to investigate how co-creation developed with highly experienced creatives involved in some of the project areas, as opposed to the 2019 experience where most of the participants had not been through such a project.

In this sense, during the period 2021–22, some online meetings were held with creators of this profile, to explore the basic requirements of this type of initiative, together with the involvement of figures with extensive experience as creators. Also during this period, contact was maintained with the co-creators of Lab 2019 with the aim of supporting them in the development of their telematics projects, once the pandemic period is over. In fact, work is underway with one of the co-creation proposals to implement their project, likely in 2023–24.

Another macro line that became evident from the perspective of the Internet (Lab features and, also the Internet as a human right and its own networked nature), lies in the need to further deepen the convergence of cultural education and educational culture. These aspects feed back into the as yet unexplored potential of e-Culture as a field of research in educational contexts. Collective creative capacities will be the link for the construction of a global culture (Ünver, 2018).

Therefore, intervention initiatives are needed that do not contain dichotomies between education and culture in order to be studied, where e-Culture itself in these contexts generates bridges and its own elaborations based on the convergence and union of both.

It is also essential to continue research into the "human factor" (Fiormonte et al, 2015) within the digital humanities as a promising field of inquiry for the basic training of society. In this sense, it is essential to integrate the training of future teachers into this field of study of technologically mediated co-creation. Since the formation of intersectoral sensitivity and creativity in body, mind, heart (Ascott, 2003) of each individual converging with technological and human mediation, are the crucial bases for co-creation, as evidenced in the operation of the Lab 2019.

To summarise, the objectives that are being researched and are underway during this year 2023, are to identify the necessary characteristics in competences and training to shape an ICT-mediated co-creation pedagogy between experienced co-creators and student teachers. In relation to a transdisciplinary approach in the field of e-Culture, interacting in the context of cultural education and educational culture.

Therefore, the Lab expands and integrates in the current new design the sphere of e-Culture as a catalytic environment in the mentioned study populations. Figure 6, illustrates the articulation of the Lab with two new integrated Lab formats, namely those related to experienced co-creators and an educational Lab focused on future teachers. In this sense, to understand the environment connecting these two target audiences, an initiative was designed to capture the situational state of the post-pandemic e-Culture. Therefore, the initiative "Global Crusade: e-Culture for all" was launched at the end of 2022, convening experts around the world (https://rb.gy/iwp7j), with the aim to make a

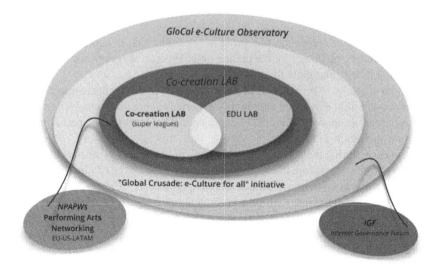

Fig. 6. Conceptual visualisation of the Lab design and research 2023–24.

"Global Statement" and with the strategy for gathering the sensitive humankind around the globe. Collecting their testimonies about two questions: 1) What is e-Culture for you?, and 2) What is your vision about e-Culture's future? This local and global endeavour has a co-creative and collaborative approach to contribute,-after the pandemic period where the culture and the e-Culture fields have been negatively affected-, for the good of humankind, making sense and engaging within the ICT benefits.

Although the Manifesto "Culture for Future" (2019), promoted by the European Commission, to which Anilla Cultural Uruguay contributed content, established promising guidelines including co-creation as relevant among other aspects of technological mediation in culture. These were perceived as slowed down or not so prospective due to the pandemic period, and the contributors to the global crusade have provided other critical views on e-Culture. In this sense, the relevance of the proposal lies in expanding and integrating research into the area of e-Culture.

During the current year 2023, the "Global Crusade" will continue while ICT analysis tools are being used to produce a global statement, along with studying individual discourses and also organising a second roundup to increase the contributions. This process will gradually shape a GloCal (global and local) e-Culture Observatory to provide continuity in the medium and long term. As a strategy, it will also seek to feed back the Lab's interventions and results to two communities (local and global), namely the Internet-based performing arts network (Europe, US and its global networks https://npa pws.org/) and the Internet Governance communities, which are the vehicle for the IGF (https://www.intgovforum.org/en) Internet Governance Forum.

In a global sense of the project from a research-based conceptual elaboration approach, a synthesis has been extracted and is explained below. Observing the trajectory and characteristics of the Lab's co-creative journey over the years, it is clear that there is a need for careful preparation of each stage of the creative process. Together with a systematic search for personalised adaptation of this process. Throughout the co-creative journey there has been a constant testing, trial, error management, adjustment, fine-tuning, as an artistic or almost artisanal practice of preparation for the different virtual or physical scenarios of co-creation. All these characteristics can be compared to the co-creative process itself being a *toile* (such as canvas). Understanding the *toile* of co-creation as a mimetic rehearsal, as a *toile* is used in the context of haute couture in its French meaning, i.e. a fabric that simulates or is a rehearsal or the mould of the final garment and serves as a preparation for the realisation of the final high quality clothing. This idea of *toile*, applied to the laboratory, is closely linked to this liminal space of co-creation, where the body and movement of each co-creator are needed to give the *toile* its real shape. And this rehearsal, understood as a process of collective creation in itself, is what enables the know-how to make the relevant changes for the production of the final garment. The concept of the *toile*, in the research, is born from the observation of the whole process and the evolution of the laboratory from 2019 to the present day. It is a meta-reflection of this period. It takes the form of a strong conceptual core that emerges from the project's interventions and research, and which continues to be tested and characterised in the construction of its good practices.

4 Preliminary Conclusions

Co-creation in contexts of technological mediation through the Internet in a distributed way, entails a complex synchronisation and articulation of very precise plans and schedules. So that spontaneity and motivation can unfold in the participants, together with the emotions, reflection and analysis that allow them to converge in co-created intangibles. From an organisational point of view, this was achieved through the strong collaborative, co-creative and distributed work prior to the Lab, in the context of Anilla Cultural UY and its global networks (section, Background information), which allowed a basic deployment for the development of the Lab in the first edition of 2019. This intensified work during the Lab process meant that the participants were able to smooth the way for any technological, communicative or other difficulties that might arise during the different stages of the process. As evidenced by the field monitoring of the process and by the analysis of the data extracted from the different platforms, in addition to the interviews carried out and the collection of testimonies from all the members and participants of the Lab. In the text of the article, this is mentioned in the passage from the first half (for instance, in Sect. 2. Multiple Deployments with Newcomers) to the second half (sub-sections, Converging and Fertile Atmosphere for Co-creation) of the Lab and to the last section where the co-creative teams were formed (sub-section, The Fruits of Co-creation and section, Boosting to the Co-creators Practitioners).

In turn, in such technology-robust contexts, it is necessary to design actions that have a symbolic impact on potential co-creators. So that they progress as co-creators and become socially legitimised as such, along with empowering more people in this field of intervention and research. This happened, for instance, in the formation of the co-creative groups and in the final public presentation of the results, together with the evaluation by an international jury of experts. In addition to all the instances of dissemination of the Lab after the first edition, open access online repository, among others.

Fostering these symbolic acts will also enhance the value of the key role of co-creation in global and local culture through e-Culture. Thus, the boosting of professional co-creators, the generation of a characterisation of the qualities of a space suitable for co-creation (subsection, Building the co-creation house). Even the lines of intervention and research currently underway, all constitute the promotion of such symbolic acts of valorisation, substantiation and contribution of co-creation to networked e-culture.

Practising the pedagogy of co-creation in these technologically mediated environments offers promising lines of citizen training, where future teachers have a fundamental role in cultural shaping. The need for co-creation pedagogy was evident in the co-creative groups, where indirect support strategies were used so that they could see and decide for themselves which path to take in the process. Avoiding a unidirectional top-down approach from the Lab.

This type of emerging pedagogy is not understood in a normative sense to be taught. But it is necessary to maintain an attentive and active attitude towards the liminal elements that constitute it, and that by their very nature make it dynamic and mutable. For this reason, in the analysis of the whole process of the Lab from 2019 to the present day, the concept of the *toile* has been applied to the processes of collective creation. Focusing in particular on the human factor that embodies this *toile* to co-create, in other words, the relationship between its skills and tools in this process. Therefore, the role of the *toile* (and deepening its research in this context) could favour the study of this emerging pedagogy. For instance, a hypothesis for future work could focus on the linkages between the *toile* and co-creative pedagogy. In order to visualise possible qualitative and even quantitative improvements, such as in the reduction of participant drop-outs.

Maintaining this liminal stance is challenging in itself, as it positions pedagogy at its oldest roots, helping to create something new. In this liminal space, it would be appropriate to investigate the skills needed to perceive the new technologically mediated co-creation processes in a local and global correlation.

Acknowledgements. The collaboration of the NRENs of Uruguay (RAU), Mexico (CUDI), Colombia (RENATA), Ecuador (CEDIA), Brazil (RNP), of the Latin American region (Red CLARA), in the United States (Internet 2) and Europe (GARR and GÉANT), Faculty of Engineering of the UdelaR in Montevideo, The Internet House of Latin America and the Caribbean in Montevideo, and the Uruguay School of Naturopathy offered human and technological support in different areas, locations and instances of the Laboratory. We also acknowledge the contribution (2019) Translation Degree of the University of the Republic (Uruguay) for the professional practice of interpreters in Spanish, English and Portuguese languages.

Special thanks for their collaborations to the NPAPWs referents: Claudio Allocchio, Justin Trieger, Tom Gorman, Domenico Vicinanza and Ann Doyle. Also many thanks for several collaborations into the Lab to Bryan Rill and Matti Hämäläinen, Anna Dumitriu, Luján Oulton, Gabriel Lambach, Tadeus Mucelli, Marina Hanganu, Laura Moazedi and Gita Senka.

Acknowledgment for the Interpreters coordination with the technical team (Federico Brum, Alejandra González, Fernando González) and the students who performed the interpretations as part of the professional practice of the Translation Career at UdelaR University. We are grateful for the remarkable collaboration of Julio Cardozo, Luis Castillo, Mariela de León, Mirta Podestá, Marcelo Parada in Uruguay; of Carlos Casasús, Martha Ávila, Eduardo Romero, Enrique Córdoba y Ollin Ibarra in Mexico; of Michael Stanton, Eduardo Grizendi, Iara Machado, Leonardo Ciuffo,

Alex Moura in Brazil; of Claudia Acosta in Colombia; of Carlos Guzmán in Ecuador; of Luis E. Cadenas, Mark Urbanin in the Latin America region.

Many thanks to Roy Ascott, Alfredo Ronchi and Halit Ünver for their generosity and openness in different consultations about their books.

Many thanks to the PhD Programme 2023 in UNIR (Spain) and acknowledgements to my tutors Raquel Gil Fernández and Carmen Escribano for the opportunity to channel this research.

Last but not least, from the Lab our special gratitude to all the participants and co-creators that attended and interacted in this experiment.

References

Anilla Cultural. http://anillacultural.net. Accessed 15 May 2023

Anilla Cultural and Latinoamérica-Europa en Uruguay y sus redes globales. Anilla Cultural UY: Latinoamérica-Europa en Uruguay y sus redes globales (2023). https://anillaculturaluruguay. net/. Accessed 15 May 2023

Anilla Cultural UY: Latinoamérica-Europa en Uruguay y sus redes globales, YouTube channel. https://www.youtube.com/@AnillaCulturalUruguay. Accessed 15 May 2023

Anilla Cultural node in Uruguay: Launching. https://rb.gy/anyyc. Accessed 15 May 2023

Ascott, R.: Telematic Embrace. Visionary, Theories of art, technology and consciousness. California, Estados Unidos: University of California Press (2003)

Baeva, L.: Values of media sphere and e-culture. Przeglad Wschodnioeuropejski **VIII**(1), 173–184 (2017). http://uwm.edu.pl/cbew/2017_8_1/Baeva.pdf. Accessed 15 May 2023

Baeva, L.: Communication in the E-Culture and Media: New Trends and Features. En R. Luppicini, The Changing Scope of Technoethics in Contemporary Society, pp. 327–342. IGI Global, Hershey (2018). https://doi.org/10.4018/978-1-5225-5094-5.ch018

Baeva, L.: Existential Aspects of the Development of E-Culture. En M. Khosrow-Pour, Advanced Methodologies and Technologies in Artificial Intelligence, Computer Simulation, and Human Computer Interaction, pp. 512–523. IGI Global, Hershey (2019). https://doi.org/10.4018/978-1-5225-7368-5

Casa de Internet de Latinoamérica y El Caribe. https://www.lacnic.net/casadeInternet. Accessed 15 May 2023

CISCO Webex Platform. https://www.webex.com/. Accessed 15 May 2023

Coalición de Derechos Humanos de Internet.: Carta de derechos humanos y principios para Internet (2015). https://derechosenInternet.com/docs/IRPC_Carta_Derechos_Humanos_Internet. pdf. Accessed 15 May 2023

Co-creation Lab, YouTube playlist. https://cutt.ly/CwqGrO44. Accessed 15 May 2023

Co-creation Lab. https://anillaculturaluruguay.net/lab-co-creacion-postulacion-a-co-creadores/. Accessed 15 May 2023

Co-creation Lab: what is? (document). https://rb.gy/e472h. Accessed 15 May 2023

Co-creation Lab: results 2019. https://cutt.ly/ywqGrIFH. Accessed 15 May 2023

Conference "Co-creation LAB" 2019–21 ~ "Non-scholar talk with tips to become creative in the academic life", 21st April 2021, Internet 2, Ann Arbor, Michigan USA. https://youtu.be/qUx Jb1azTqU. Accessed 15 May 2023

Conference "Cocreación en arte y ciencia mediada por TIC para la construcción de una cultura GloCal" realizada en la Universidad de Valencia "Centro Cultural La Nau, 7 Noviembre 2019. https://bit.ly/2S4hNZF. Accessed 15 May 2023

Conference "Co-creators over Internet", April, 2018. https://vimeo.com/282518942. Accessed 15 May 2023

"Crusade: e-Culture for all" Initiative, YouTube Playlist (2022–23). https://rb.gy/iwp7j. Accessed 15 May 2023

Fiormonte, D. et al.: The Digital Humanist: A Critical Inquiry. Punctum Books (2015). https://monoskop.org/images/d/dd/Fiormonte_Numerico_Tomasi_The_Digital_Humanist_A_Critical_Inquiry_2015.pdf. Accessed 15 May 2023

Harris, M.: Antropología Cultural. Alianza. España (1998)

IGF Internet Governance Forum. https://www.intgovforum.org/en

ITU-T, "H323. SERIES H: AUDIOVISUAL AND MULTIMEDIA SYSTEMS, 3/2022. https://www.itu.int/rec/T-REC-H.323-202203-I/en. Accessed 15 May 2023

Manifesto "Culture for Future", 16–19 Junio 2019. https://culturexchange.eu/system/files/2020-12/Manifesto%20Culture4Future_Annexes_0.pdf. Accessed 15 May 2023

National Research and Education Networks. https://about.geant.org/nrens/. Accessed 15 May 2023

Networking Performance Art Production. https://npapws.org. Accessed 15 May 2023

Pexip Platform. https://www.pexip.com. Accessed 15 May 2023

Rill, B.R., Hämäläinen, M.M.: The Art of Co-creation. A guide book of practitioners. Singapur: Palgrave Macmillan (2018)

Rodriguez Morales, D.: Anilla Cultural Latinoamérica-Europa en Uruguay: un análisis evolutivo con estudio de casos sobre la interacción e inclusión participativa para la cocreación en redes de Internet avanzado. Desde su fundación hasta la actualidad. En RedCLARA, ACTAS TICAL 2016, pp. 618–634 (2016). http://documentas.redclara.net/handle/10786/1237. Accessed 15 May 2023

Rodriguez Morales, D.: e-Cultura: desde una cartografía para navegantes de Internet avanzado a la formación docente de Uruguay. In: Huerta, R., Alonso-Sanz, A. (eds.) Entornos informales para educar en artes, pp. 137–145. Valencia: Publicaciones de la Universidad de Valencia (2017)

Rodriguez Morales, D.: MuRe, museografia en xarxa. REIRE Revista d'Innovació I Recerca En Educació **13**(1), 1–19 (2020). https://doi.org/10.1344/reire2020.13.128684

Ronchi, A.M.: eCulture. Cultural Content in the Digital Age. Alemania: Springer (2009)

Ronchi, A.: Human factor, resilience, and cyber/hybrid influence. Inf. Secur. J. **53**(2), 221–239 (2022). Accessed January 15, 2023, https://doi.org/10.11610/isij.5315

Ünver, H.: Global Networking, Communication and Culture: Conflict or Convergence?: Spread of ICT, Internet Governance, Superorganism Humanity and Global Culture. Springer, Alemania (2018)

Zoom Platform https://zoom.us/

Technology in Education

Exploring Women's Role in Creative Industries Through Collaborative Action Research Using Tabletop Role-Playing Games

Digdem Sezen[1][(✉)], Atakan Akcali[2], Tonguc Ibrahim Sezen[1], Sarah Perks[2], and Paul Stewart[2]

[1] University for the Creative Arts, Farnham, UK
{digdem.sezen,tonguc.sezen}@uca.ac.uk
[2] Teesside University, Middlesbrough, UK
{a.akcali,s.perks,p.stewart}@tees.ac.uk

Abstract. This paper examines the use of tabletop role-playing games (TRPGs) as a collaborative action research (CAR) tool to investigate the role of women in the creative industries of the North East region in the UK. TRPGs offer an interactive and structured platform for participants to engage in scenario-based simulations, problem-solving activities, and decision-making exercises. Through immersive experiences, TRPGs enable participants to gain insights into the challenges, constraints, and dynamics of the creative industry. The study presents the application of TRPGs in a workshop called "Agents of Equality and Empowerment", involving professionals, freelancers, students, academics, and NGO workers from the creative sectors. By assuming the roles of women creatives in TRPG scenarios, participants investigated issues like brain drain, motherhood, childcare, networking, connections, pay gap, and lack of role models. The workshop aimed to identify necessary changes, understand priorities, and explore the subjective experiences of women creatives in the North East. Findings derived from surveys, qualitative analysis of in-game interactions, observations, and reflections shed light on practical aspects and emotional dimensions of women's involvement in the creative industries. This understanding facilitates a deeper exploration of barriers, biases, societal expectations, and cultural influences that shape their professional journeys.

Keywords: Collaborative Action Research · Tabletop Role Playing Games · Creative Industries · Women Creatives · North East UK

1 Introduction

This paper explores the application of tabletop role-playing games (TRPGs) as a tool for collaborative action research (CAR), focusing on understanding women's role in creative industries in the North East of the UK. TRPGs provide an interactive and structured environment for participants to engage in scenario-based simulations, problem-solving activities, and decision-making exercises. By simulating real-world situations

D. Crawford et al. (Eds.): TIE 2023, LNICST 575, pp. 39–53, 2024.
https://doi.org/10.1007/978-3-031-59383-3_3

and complex systems, TRPGs allow participants to gain insights into the challenges, constraints, and dynamics of the creative industry. The immersive nature of TRPGs promotes experiential exchange, reflection, and creative problem-solving.

In this study, TRPGs were applied as a tool to explore the women's role in creative industries in the North East of the UK in a workshop. Agents of Equality and Empowerment Workshop involved professionals, freelancers, students, academics, and NGO workers in the creative sectors. Through role-playing exercises and discussions within the game, participants explored various issues such as brain drain, motherhood, childcare, networking, connections, pay gap, and lack of role models. The workshop aimed to identify what needs to change, understand priorities, and explore the subjective experiences of women creatives in the region. By assuming the roles of women creatives within the TRPG scenarios, participants were able to immerse themselves in the challenges, triumphs, and complexities of being a woman creative in the North East UK. The findings from the workshop gathered through surveys and qualitative analysis of in-game interactions, observations, and reflections, shed light on the practical aspects as well as the emotional dimensions of women's role in creative industries. This understanding allowed for a deeper exploration of the barriers, biases, societal expectations, and cultural factors that shape their professional journeys.

2 Using Tabletop Role-Playing Games as a Tool for Collaborative Action Research

CAR is a research approach that aims to address real-world problems and improve practices through a process of inquiry, reflection, and action [1]. In CAR, researchers work closely with practitioners or community members to identify an issue or a problem that needs to be addressed. The research process involves collaborative planning, data collection, analysis, and interpretation, and the development and implementation of action plans based on the findings [2]. CAR involves active participation and collaboration among various stakeholders in a particular field or community, such as researchers, practitioners, community members, policymakers, and relevant parties [3]. The emphasis is on shared ownership of the research process and outcomes. It is action-oriented, aiming to bring about positive change or improvement in a specific context by engaging in problem-solving and implementing actions based on research findings [4]. Reflective inquiry is an integral part of collaborative action research, involving a cyclical process of critical examination, knowledge generation, and continuous reflection on the effectiveness of actions taken [5]. This type of research recognizes the significance of understanding local contexts, cultural nuances, and unique challenges to develop solutions that are relevant to the specific context or community [6]. It also values the participation and input of all stakeholders, aiming to empower and provide agency to individuals. By creating a democratic and inclusive research environment, CAR ensures that diverse perspectives and voices are heard and valued [7]. By actively involving practitioners and stakeholders, collaborative action research seeks to bridge the gap between theory and practice, generate practical knowledge, and promote sustainable change within the targeted setting. It is often employed in fields such as education [8], healthcare [9], community development [10] and organizational development [11], where there is a need to address complex problems and improve practices in collaboration with those directly involved.

TRPGs can be used as a valuable tool in CAR, providing a structured and interactive environment for participants to engage in scenario-based simulations, problem-solving activities, and decision-making exercises. These games offer a range of benefits that align with the principles of CAR, such as active participation, experiential learning, and collective problem-solving. By simulating real-world situations or complex systems, TRPGs allow participants to explore and understand the intricacies of a particular context [12]. By assuming different roles and interacting with the game environment, participants can gain insights into the challenges, constraints, and dynamics that exist within the targeted setting [13]. This hands-on experience enables a deeper understanding of the issues at hand. The immersive nature of TRPGs promotes experiential exchange, enabling participants to experiment with different strategies, make decisions, and observe the consequences of their actions within the game. As a result, participants can reflect on their assumptions, biases, and practices, leading to deeper insights and potential shifts in thinking. Moreover, TRPGs inherently foster collaboration and teamwork [14]. Participants must work together, often assuming different roles or characters, to achieve common goals or solve problems within the game. This collaborative element mirrors the nature of action research, where multiple stakeholders collaborate to bring about positive change. The teamwork within TRPGs builds a sense of collective ownership and facilitates a shared understanding of the research objectives. In addition to collaboration, TRPGs stimulate creative problem-solving. These games often present complex challenges or dilemmas that require participants to think critically, analyse information, and generate innovative solutions. Furthermore, TRPGs provide a safe and controlled environment for participants to experiment with different approaches or strategies without real-world consequences [15]. This fosters a culture of experimentation and learning, allowing participants to explore new ideas, test hypotheses, and evaluate potential interventions. The safe space provided by TRPGs encourages participants to take risks and think outside the box [16]. Lastly, the data generated from TRPG sessions, including participant observations, in-game interactions, decision-making processes, and reflections, can be recorded, observed, and analysed for research purposes [17]. This data can inform the research process, validate findings, or identify areas for improvement. Incorporating TRPGs in CAR can enhance participant engagement, facilitates experiential exchange, stimulates collective problem-solving, and generates valuable insights for research and practice. Designing and facilitating TRPG sessions in a way that aligns with the research objectives, maintains ethical considerations, and ensures the active involvement of all participants is crucial for success.

In order to put this methodology to the test, we organized a workshop as part of the Creative Fuse project at Teesside University with the aim of exploring women's experiences in creative industries in the North East UK. Understanding women's experiences within the creative industries is crucial for fostering inclusivity and ensuring equal opportunities. Therefore, by incorporating TRPGs into CAR approach during the workshop, we aimed to delve deeper into the unique challenges and triumphs faced by women in the North East UK's creative sector. This innovative methodology allowed us to witness firsthand the impact it had on participant engagement, providing valuable insights into how TRPGs can facilitate meaningful discussions and empower women in driving growth and innovation within the industry.

3 Understanding Women's Role in Creative Industries in the North East UK

The creative industries are a vital component of the UK's economy, generating billions of pounds each year and offering job opportunities to hundreds of thousands of individuals across a diverse range of sectors, such as advertising, architecture, crafts, design, fashion, film, video, music, performing arts, publishing, museums, galleries, libraries, IT, software, and computer games [18]. While both men and women have made significant contributions to these industries, it is crucial to acknowledge and empower the essential role of women in driving growth, innovation, and overall success within the sector and the UK economy.

Numerous studies by industry experts and academics have examined women's experiences and representation in the creative industries. The 2021 DCMS Creative Industries report found that women comprise 38.0% of the workforce [19]. The Creative Media and Entertainment Sector Skills Assessment report of 2012 highlighted the underrepresentation of women across nearly all sectors of the creative media industries, citing the challenge of balancing family life with unpredictable work hours as a contributing factor [20]. In the United Kingdom film industry during 2020, women accounted for only 26% of screenwriters and 23% of directors, according to the British Film Institute's 2021 yearbook [21]. Directors UK's Gender Equality Report of 2018 found that only 25% of TV episodes broadcast were directed by women [22]. Additionally, the UK Games Census Diversity Report of 2021 showed that only 30% of individuals surveyed identified as female, with 3% identifying as non-binary or other, indicating a significant disparity in gender representation within the games workforce [23]. In 2016, a Young Creative Council survey found that male creative directors made up 96.4% of the sector, and 88% of young female creatives expressed a lack of female role models, with 70% never having worked with a female creative or executive director [24].

Although the creative industries are particularly strong in London, other regions of the UK, such as the North East, have developed their unique creative scenes. According to DCMS official statistics, the creative industries accounted for 3.2% of all jobs in the North East region in 2015 [25]. NESTA and Creative England identified Middlesbrough and Stockton as high-growth creative clusters in the North East in their 2016 report [26]. The North East's cultural and creative industries exhibit distinct working practices and behaviours, which are contained within the region and physically and cognitively separated from the larger concentration of cultural and creative industries based in London and face several challenges when trying to engage with those outside their local area, such as limited financial and time resources and lack of knowledge [27].

In recent years, there have been efforts to address gender discrimination, lack of representation, access to funding, and limited opportunities for career progression and promote greater gender diversity and inclusion in the creative industries of the North East. For instance, initiatives such as Women in Tech North East was established to support and promote women's involvement in digital and technology sectors [28]. Boldly Grow, as part of the Creative Fuse Tees Valley, offers business planning workshops and seminars to support women artists, creatives, and business leaders in the Tees Valley [28]. The North East Cultural Freelancers initiative actively campaigns for the protection of freelance workers' rights, advocates for their well-being, generates new opportunities and raises awareness of the often-overlooked contributions made by freelance labourers within the cultural sector of the North East region [29].

4   Creative Collaboration Through TRPGs: Agents of Equality and Empowerment Workshop

Building on the ongoing efforts to promote gender diversity and inclusion in the creative industries of the North East, for our study, we employed a creative collaboration approach to further explore women's role in creativity and innovation. In line with these objectives, we organised a workshop titled "Agents of Equality and Empowerment", hosted at Teesside University. It aimed to bring together a diverse range of participants, including professionals, freelancers, decision-makers, students, academics, and NGO workers in the creative sectors, to gather valuable insights and experiences. As a half-day workshop, it provided a platform for exchanging ideas and fostering dialogue.

The sample group for the women's workshop comprised 10 participants from various backgrounds and experiences. All participants were provided with information about the study and gave their informed consent to participate. The workshop was recorded with the participants' written consent, and their identities were kept anonymous during the analysis. The materials created by the participants were scanned for analysis, and a survey designed to elicit information on the participants' experiences was administered after the workshop. The data was kept confidential and used only for the purposes of the research. A disclaimer was included stating that the characters and scenarios in the workshop were fictional and that any resemblance to real people or situations was coincidental. The purpose of the workshop was to explore creative industry-related issues and develop strategies through role-playing exercises. The organizers and facilitators did not endorse discriminatory or harmful behaviour towards individuals or groups.

The workshop was structured as a TRPG-inspired collective playful prototyping session following CAR principles. The participants were assigned one of 25 pre-generated personas representing different stakeholders in creative industries and challenges faced by women in these industries, each with personal goals, some of which at odds with each other. These pre-generated characters had standardized features consisting of a name, gender, age, position within the creative industries, emotions towards their job, opinions and reactions towards gender roles in creative industries, challenges they face, desires and fears they have, and in some cases contradictions in their world views.

ChatGPT (GPT-3.5) is used without any additional training as a supportive tool during the development of these fictional characters. Prompts were used to create flawed and biased characters, drawing inspiration from real-life experiences and the themes and context of the workshop. Thus, concepts like glass ceilings or gender pay gap are inserted into character creation prompts. However, ChatGPT rejected the creation of characters with negative tendencies or biases towards women's role in creative industries. The prompts were modified by removing directly negative descriptions. These changes led to the creation of more conflicting PCs and NPCs to which ChatGPT attributed both positive and negative characteristics. For example, a character in a senior position who preferred to hire women who don't have children and rationalizing this within the context of the needs of her organisation became, after modifications, someone who believes that women can achieve success in creative leadership roles, but also holds the view that women who have children might not be as dedicated to their careers and may be less reliable as team members. Thus, characters were improved by introducing internal conflicts, which formed the basis for discussion and discovery during the workshop. Other difficulties faced during the ChatGPT-aided preparation phase included the lack of representation of disabilities and limited binary gender options. Manual adjustments were made to address these limitations, including gender orientations, disabilities, and diverse backgrounds.

The workshop began with participants forming randomly selected smaller groups, personal introductions, and the distribution of name tags containing their real names and, later, their fictional characters' names. The name tag element added to the immersive atmosphere and further emphasised the distinction between their real-life identity and the character they embodied. Each participant then received a game pack consisting of a brief explanation of role-playing, one of the above-described character profiles, and an introductory narrative describing their overall mission, the development of a regional "Women's Creative Hub" as a group, which had to have certain functions related to the roles of women in creative industries. Fifteen minutes were given for participants to familiarise themselves with their in-game characters. During that time, they were also encouraged to find three commonalities with their group members to enhance the embodiment phase based on their in-game character's features.

To ensure fairness and avoid promoting any particular narrative, we distributed the pre-prepared game packs randomly to the groups. The game packs were designed to create a discussion environment by including contradicting characters without creating toxic game mechanics promoting unhealthy behaviour or creating frustration in terms of gameplay. Participants were given three sub-missions and given thirty minutes to complete each task. The missions focused on different aspects of the creation of the Creative Hub and its objectives. Overall, the workshop was structured mostly in a collective storytelling format without direct supervision, but random pre-generated challenges and supportive trends were introduced throughout the workshop by the organizers.

The provided narrative presents a fictional scenario that mirrors real-world challenges women face in the creative industries, including brain drain to larger cities, motherhood and childcare responsibilities, networking difficulties, lack of role models, and limited funding and resources. Despite these obstacles, the narrative depicts women determined to establish a Creative Hub in Teesside, which would offer support, resources, and networking opportunities to women in the creative industries and contribute to the growth and diversity of the sector in the region. In Mission 1, participants conducted an introduction and needs assessment for the Creative Hub. This involved finding a suitable brand, including a name and a logo for the hub, providing an overview of the initiative, discussing the specific needs of professional women in creative industries, and outlining the challenges faced by women creatives in the community.

The first team chose the name "Checit" for their hub, which stands for Creative Hub for Economic and Cultural Values in Teesside. This group, considering their personas, placed importance on addressing various challenges, including the exodus of talented individuals to larger cities, limited networking opportunities, sentimental attachment to Teesside, a scarcity of mentors and role models, and unstable working conditions. The in-game personas consist primarily of creative individuals in their twenties who work in fields such as advertising and IT, as well as students in creative sectors. By discussing the common needs of their personas, they proposed the concept of a hub that would facilitate local and external mentorship for young professionals, foster connections with local business owners, and secure funding to establish a dedicated, inclusive space and resources for skill development.

The second team, the Shield Hub, comprises a diverse range of personas. Among them are a female freelance designer juggling childcare responsibilities, a male CEO of a marketing agency, a 45-year-old female senior creative director, and a 40-year-old male film director. These personas collectively identified brain drain to larger cities, childcare responsibilities, and precarious work conditions as the primary challenges faced by professionals in the regional creative sectors. In response, they put forth the concept of the Shield Hub, which aims to establish a secure and inclusive environment for networking and collaboration among junior and senior creatives within the local sector. The hub would provide essential support such as childcare facilities and workspace assistance, enabling professionals to overcome these challenges effectively.

The third group, named Saraswati, comprises three distinct personas. It includes a seasoned male art director with extensive industry expertise, a dedicated female senior designer, and a young freelance designer in their twenties seeking networking opportunities. The team's primary focus revolved around addressing challenges related to employment disparities, unstable work conditions and overall uncertainty in creative sectors. The initial mission enabled player participants to fully immerse themselves in their unique fictional identities, fostering a deeper understanding of their fellow players' personas while collectively clarifying their shared goals.

Mission 2 centred around establishing the objectives and action plan for the Creative Hub. Participants were required to define the hub's vision, mission, and values and set long-term goals for professional women in the creative industries. They also had to explain how the hub planned to empower and support women. Strategies for inclusivity, diversity, collaboration with other organisations, and staying abreast of industry trends were discussed. The Checit team has defined their mission as a catalyst for aspiring creative professionals, investing in the concept of fostering a sense of belonging within the Teesside community. Their primary objective is to establish an inclusive environment for young creatives, where they can receive support and encouragement to cultivate strong local relationships with fellow creatives, local businesses, and mentors. The team places particular emphasis on leveraging digital platforms to facilitate this vision. They recognize that their creative hub model extends beyond physical space, as they intend to develop a digital ecosystem for community building, skill development, business networking, and long-term sustainability. By actively nurturing a sense of belonging and continuously investing in their mission, they aim to foster a sustainable relationship between experienced creative professionals and newcomers to the field.

The Shield Hub team extensively deliberated on how the hub can effectively support creatives with migrant backgrounds. Comprising individuals from diverse backgrounds themselves, the team recognized the importance of inclusivity and actively sought to create a space that catered to people of various age groups, genders, ethnicities, and cultural backgrounds, including those with disabilities. Their vision for the hub included essential amenities such as a café, green area, and a dedicated kids' area, aiming to foster connections among local creatives and facilitate collaborations with external groups both within the UK and on an international scale. The team's comprehensive approach considered not only the physical attributes of the space but also the pivotal role it played in providing women with a supportive platform to freely express themselves, free from bias and filled with encouragement.

The third group, Saraswati, presented highly pragmatic and commercially viable models to generate income. Their proposals included establishing local partnerships with institutions such as Teesside University to offer accredited training courses and internship agreements with prominent local media companies like BBC Sunderland. Instead of relying solely on government funding, they suggested forming partnerships with local businesses and implementing a membership plan for the various components of the creative hub. Recognizing the significance of connectivity, they explored sponsorship agreements with internet service providers to offer free Wi-Fi within the hub. Additionally, they aimed to introduce TEDx-like events to support inspirational activities in the region. Through sponsorships, they aspired to collaborate with companies such as Adobe to equip the hub with industry-standard software. The team also displayed ambition in creating nationally recognized accredited training programs and qualifications exclusively for their members, further enhancing the professional development opportunities within the hub.

Lastly, in Mission 3, participants were asked to create a timeline for the hub's development and a marketing and promotion strategy. They also had to devise a sustainable funding plan and strategic timeline for the launch of the Creative Hub, ensuring long-term success and impact through diverse funding sources and partnerships. The Checit team, driven by their investment in the concept of belonging, heavily relies on donations and alumni grants to sustain their proposed business model for the hub. They put forth a sustainable approach centred around a continuous cycle of mentors. Their primary objective is to nurture a sense of belonging and enhance the hub's digital ecosystem. According to their model, successful creative professionals who have benefited from the hub will contribute back by providing digital or in-person support to newcomers. This alumni model establishes a strong foundation built on the idea of belonging, ensuring that regardless of their future endeavours, these creatives will maintain connections with the hub and have the opportunity to mentor new members. The Shield Hub team generated innovative concepts for organizing fundraising activities within the hub's inviting and appealing space. Their goal was to garner support from globally recognized institutions and orchestrate international exhibitions that would connect local artists with their counterparts worldwide. They emphasized that this initiative would provide creatives with a unique opportunity to gain intimate insights into how artists in other countries navigate similar challenges. The Saraswati group, while initially considering government funding, aims to establish a sustainable model that does not solely rely on it. They devised a membership plan designed for both creatives and local business owners who will utilize the hub's facilities. By bringing these groups together, the hub will serve as a vibrant meeting place and foster collaboration. To promote the hub, the team intends to employ a multi-channel approach, utilizing online platforms as well as advertising in industry journals and business media. Additionally, they recognize the importance of reaching a wider audience and plan to distribute physical copies to effectively engage with people.

Throughout the workshop, opportunity, crisis, and trend cards were assigned randomly to groups to enhance the playfulness and engagement of the role-playing method. These cards introduced various scenarios and challenges that mirrored real-world situations faced by women in the creative industries. Each card prompted the groups to consider how they would respond or navigate the given challenges. The cards included economic recessions affecting funding and job security, political instability limiting creative expression, climate change disrupting supply chains, technological advancements automating specific creative jobs, increasing competition from emerging markets, shifts in social and cultural values, health crises impacting work and collaboration, changing consumer preferences, rising costs of living, and workplace discrimination. These cards aimed to encourage the participants to think critically and develop strategies to address the challenges faced by women in the creative industries with a specific focus on digital innovations and trends. The participants, who were digital media students, were able to relate to these scenarios more closely due to their background and familiarity with digital technologies. The others developed ideas based on their coping strategies through the COVID-19 pandemic. The cards stimulated discussions and decision-making processes within the groups, fostering a dynamic and immersive role-playing experience. Additionally, the cards incorporated opportunities and trends in the creative industry, such as technological advancements, diversity and inclusivity, economy and freelance work, global market access, sustainability, and ethical practices.

During the role-play, participants had engaging interactions that led to memorable experiences for everyone involved. The process of embodying the fictional personas brought about fun moments for the groups. For instance, real-life freelance creatives took on the roles of senior characters with vast industry experience. Some participants who typically did not have caregiving responsibilities had to navigate the challenges of childcare, while others who were parents in real life portrayed senior creative directors balancing work priorities. An interesting dynamic emerged when one of the players, a professional in their 50s, was assigned the role of a young freelancer, while her group members, who were in their 20s in real life, portrayed experienced professionals. Throughout the session, it was evident that despite the age difference, the 50+ player's character accurately understood the experiences of late-career professionals. Taking on a leadership role, she played a key part in establishing the project's goals. The final project presented by the group stood out as the most comprehensive and well-structured proposal, with a strong focus on organizational and financial aspects.

The players' real-life identities, needs, hopes, and expectations often intertwined with those of their fictional characters, even though the characters they portrayed were significantly different from their own personalities. They also incorporated their personal real-life problems, fears, and expectations when advocating for their characters during arguments. In cases where the character differed from their real-life persona in terms of gender, job role, or sector, it presented certain challenges to fully embody the character. At times, players expressed a desire to abandon their character. Their motivation for abandoning the character was to express how they really feel about the situation in real life based on their own experiences in creative sector. In such instances, workshop organizers intervened and redirected their focus back to the game. Even though the player first complied with these requests, after a while, they merged their real-life experiences with the given persona's. Such concept of emotions, thoughts, relationships, and physical states extending beyond the boundaries of the game environment is referred to as "bleed" in TRPG literature [30]. In addition, it is possible for players to aim for a strategy known as "Close to Home", where they intentionally try to weaken the protective structure of the play [31], and this was observed when the player who is in their 50s took on the role of a young freelancer and utilised their expertise to their advantage in the role-play.

Overall, the utilization of diverse characters allowed the players to embody various perceptions of professionals in the creative sector, including different roles, genders, and sectors. Players not only provided solutions to in-game problems based on their character's perspective but also drew from their personal experiences, education, and backgrounds to offer additional insights. The participants generally reacted positively to the challenges provided by the organisers, and from the outset, they demonstrated a deep understanding of the interconnected challenges faced by women in the region.

5 Follow-Up Survey Analysis

A follow-up survey (n = 10) was conducted after the workshop to gather comprehensive information about participants' experiences. Utilizing Microsoft Forms, participants rated their agreement on a scale of 1 to 5, with one being strongly disagree and five being strongly agree. The collected data underwent quantitative analysis employing descriptive statistics. The survey results showed that participants best described their field in creative industries: film, TV, video, radio and photography; design; advertising and marketing; IT, software and computer services; and publishing. Most participants (n = 6) had 1 to 6 years of experience in creative industries. The participants were also asked whether they had played a role-playing game before, with three participants responding positively.

The survey first focused on how the participants perceived the game characters they were assigned to. The participants were asked if the characters they embodied during the role-playing workshop represented their real-life identities. The average rating for this question was 2.00, indicating a lower level of agreement. This suggests that, on average, participants felt that the character they embodied during the workshop did not closely align with their real-life identity. Although these characters were written to mirror real-life problems, they also had diverse thoughts about the creative industries to represent different stakeholders. These added depth and complexity to the role-playing experience, allowing participants to explore different perspectives and engage with the nuances of the creative industry challenges. Similarly, when participants were asked to provide their agreement regarding whether they played a role different from their own identity, the average rating was 3.88, indicating moderate agreement. This suggests that participants acknowledged the disparity between their assigned character and their real identity, highlighting the transformative nature of the role-playing experience. The divergence between their persona and their embodied role likely facilitated the exploration of unique perspectives and behaviours, fostering an immersive environment for personal growth and self-exploration.

To explore the role-playing experience itself, the participants were asked to evaluate if they could maintain the persona of the character they were assigned to during the workshop. The average rating for this question was 3.63, indicating a moderate level of agreement. This could suggest that while participants made an effort to embody their assigned character, there may have been some challenges in fully maintaining the persona throughout the exercise. The relatively lower rating could imply that additional support, such as props or visual cues, could enhance the participants' embodiment of their characters and further immerse them in the role-playing experience. Furthermore, when asked whether participants felt challenged when their real personality and assigned character contradicted each other, the average rating of 3.88 suggests a moderate agreement. This indicates that some individuals experienced a level of conflict or tension when embodying a character that differed from their own personality. However, the results also revealed that participants strongly agreed (4.50 average rating) with the statement that role-playing as someone else during the workshop provided them with a platform to express ideas and opinions they might not have felt comfortable sharing as themselves. Hence, it could be argued that the role-playing method created a safe and non-judgmental environment where participants felt empowered to explore perspectives and viewpoints they may have otherwise hesitated to express, fostering a greater sense of freedom and creativity and enabling open and uninhibited discussions during the workshop.

To find out how the role-playing experience contributed to their understanding of the creative industries, the participants were asked whether they discovered something new about their real personalities while acting as their given character. The participants responded positively, with an average rating of 4.63. Even though the sample size was small, this could suggest that the immersive nature of the role-playing method provided an opportunity for self-reflection and self-analysis, enabling individuals to gain insights into their own thoughts, behaviours, and characteristics through the lens of their role-played character. Participants were also asked to rate their agreement with the statement, "Participating in this role-playing workshop provided you with a fresh outlook or understanding on your personal life or past encounters as a creative individual". The average rating for this question was 4.75, indicating a high level of agreement. This suggests that the role-playing workshop significantly impacted participants' perspectives and understanding of their personal life and past experiences as creative individuals. The immersive nature of the workshop that utilised the role-playing method likely allowed participants to explore different scenarios and challenges, leading to new insights and a fresh outlook on their creative journey. Finally, participants were asked to rate their agreement with the statements regarding the limitation of opportunities or potentials based on their gender in real life and the role-playing workshop. In real life, the average rating for this question was 4.13, indicating a relatively high level of agreement that gender has indeed had an impact on opportunities and potentials in the creative industry. In the role-playing workshop, however, the average rating for the same question was 3.38, suggesting a slightly lower level of agreement. These findings suggest that while participants recognised the impact of gender on opportunities and potentials in the creative industry in real life, the role-playing exercise may have provided a different perspective or allowed for a more nuanced exploration of these dynamics.

Finally, the survey explored the perception of the incorporation of opportunity, crisis, and trend cards in the workshop, which aimed to increase the fun and engagement of the role-playing method while giving relevant context for real-life issues. Participants were then asked to rate how these cards affected their overall enjoyment of the role-playing experience. According to the ratings, the opportunity cards had a significant impact on enjoyment, receiving an average rating of 4.75. The crisis cards also positively influenced enjoyment, with an average rating of 4.25. Although the trend cards received a slightly lower average rating of 4.13, they still contributed to participants' overall enjoyment. These findings indicate that including these cards contributed to the engaging and enjoyable nature of the role-playing experience.

Although the study was limited by a small sample size, the utilisation of the role-play method was observed to have a positive impact on participants' personal growth and self-exploration as creative individuals. Embodying a different persona allowed for the exploration of unique perspectives and behaviours in a more immersive environment. Through this activity, participants engaged in self-reflection and analysis, gaining insights into their own thoughts, behaviours, and characteristics through the lens of their role-played character. This suggests that role-play can be an effective tool for individuals seeking to gain a greater understanding of themselves and their personal experiences.

6   Conclusion

In conclusion, the TRPG sessions provided a platform for experiential exchange, allowing participants to immerse themselves in creative narratives and engage with one another in a dynamic and interactive manner. This not only stimulated collective problem-solving but also generated valuable insights for both research and practice. However, we acknowledge that the success of such sessions relies heavily on careful design and facilitation. To fully leverage the transformative potential of tabletop role-playing games (TRPGs) in addressing complex challenges within creative industries, it is essential to approach each session with clear research objectives in mind. In addition, ethical considerations must be taken into account, and all participants should be actively involved in the planning and execution of the game. By adopting this approach, everyone involved can benefit from the unique problem-solving capabilities a CAR approach inspired by TRPGs offers. By creating a structured and inclusive environment, participants can explore issues from multiple perspectives, gain insights that might not be apparent through traditional research methods and develop a deeper understanding of the challenges at hand. Ultimately, this approach can lead to more effective and impactful solutions that can help drive positive change within the creative industries.

The study also provided insights on how to use language models like ChatGPT in TRPG design. Our research has shown that such systems can be used to create characters for serious role-playing experiences. While language models' adherence to ethical principles makes the inclusion of flawed PCs and NPCs challenging, modifications made in character development to overcome this challenge can add further dimensions to fictional characters, advancing their playability. The presence of biases such as binary gender representation and limitations in diverse character development despite updated prompts indicates the need for further development and refinement of the process, however. Overall, the positive impact on participants' self-exploration using characters created with the aid of ChatGPT highlights the potential of language models in TRPG writing.

By acknowledging the subjective experiences and emotions of women creatives, the study contributes to a comprehensive understanding of the challenges they face and the support they require. This knowledge forms a basis for developing strategies and interventions that foster gender diversity, inclusion, and empowerment in the creative industries of the North East UK. It enables policymakers, practitioners, and stakeholders to design targeted initiatives that address both the practical and emotional aspects of supporting women creatives in their professional development, ultimately creating a more inclusive and supportive ecosystem for their success. Overall, the use of TRPGs in collaborative action research has shown to be a promising approach for gaining a deeper understanding of complex issues and generating practical knowledge that can be applied in both research and real-world settings. By engaging in such activities, researchers and participants are able to explore these issues in a safe and constructive environment while also gaining valuable insights that can inform future research and decision-making. Ultimately, this approach can lead to more effective and innovative solutions to pressing social and environmental challenges.

References

1. Riel, M.: Understanding Collaborative Action Research. http://base.socioeco.org/docs/cen ter_for_collaborative_action_research.pdf. Accessed 23 May 2023
2. Enomoto, E.: Book review: how to conduct collaborative action research. Int. J. Educ. Reform **3**, 361–363 (1994)
3. Gordon, S.P.: Collaborative Action Research: Developing Professional Learning Communities. Teachers College Press, New York (2008)
4. Wicks, P., Reason, P., Bradbury, H. (eds.): The SAGE Handbook of Action Research. 2nd: SAGE Publications Ltd (2008). https://doi.org/10.4135/9781848607934. Accessed 23 May 2023
5. Ospina, S., Dodge, J., Foldy, E.G., Hofman-Pinilla, A.: Taking the action turn: lessons from bringing participation to qualitative research. In: Reason, P., Bradbury-Huang, H. (eds.) The SAGE Handbook of Action Research: Participative Inquiry and Practice, 2nd edn. SAGE Publications, London (2007)
6. McNiff, J.: Action Research: Principles and Practice. Taylor and Francis, London, UK (2013)
7. Reason, P., Bradbury-Huang, H.: Exemplars: introduction to exemplars: varieties of action research. In: Reason, P., Bradbury-Huang, H. (eds.) The SAGE Handbook of Action Research: Participative Inquiry and Practice, 2nd edn. SAGE Publications, London, UK (2007)
8. Feldman, A.: The role of conversation in collaborative action research. Educ. Action Res. **7**(1), 125–147 (1999)
9. Hughes, I.: Action research in healthcare. In: Reason, P., Bradbury-Huang, H. (eds.) The SAGE Handbook of Action Research: Participative Inquiry and Practice, 2nd edn. SAGE Publications, London (2007)

10. Penrod, J., Loeb, S.J., Ladonne, R.A., Martin, M.L.: Empowering change agents in hierarchical organizations: participatory action research in prisons. Res. Nurs. Health **39**(3), 142–153 (2016)
11. Stringer, E.: This is So Democratic! Action Research and Policy Development in East Timor, In: Reason, P., Bradbury-Huang, H. (eds.) The SAGE Handbook of Action Research: Participative Inquiry and Practice, 2nd edn. SAGE Publications, London (2007)
12. Grouling, J.: The Creation of Narrative in Tabletop Role-Playing Games, McFarland& Company, North Carolina, US (2010)
13. Ibid
14. Daniau, S.: The transformative potential of role-playing games-: from play skills to human skills. Simul. Gaming **47**(4), 423–444 (2016)
15. Dyson, S.B., Chang, Y., Chen, H., Hsiung, H., Tseng, C., Chang, J.: The effect of tabletop role-playing games on the creative potential and emotional creativity of Taiwanese college students. Thinking Skills Creativity **19**, 88–96 (2016)
16. Poeller, S., Dechant, M., Mandryk, R.L.: Playing a flawless character? exploring differences between experts and novices in tabletop role-playing games and potential benefits for well-being. In: FDG'23: Proceedings of the 18th International Conference on the Foundations of Digital Games, pp. 1–7 (2023)
17. Tychsen, A., Newman, K., Brolund, T., Hitchens, M.: Cross-format analysis of the gaming experience in multi-player role-playing games, Situated Play, Proceedings of DiGRA 2007 Conference. https://www.academia.edu/download/40978345/07311.39029.pdf. Accessed 23 May 2023
18. Creative Industries Mapping Documents 2001. https://www.gov.uk/government/publications/creative-industries-mapping-documents-2001. Accessed 23 May 2023
19. DCMS Sectors Economic Estimates: Workforce, January to December 2021. https://www.gov.uk/government/statistics/dcms-sector-economic-estimates-workforce-2021/dcms-sectors-economic-estimates-workforce-january-to-december-2021. Accessed 23 May 2023
20. UK Commission for Employment and Skills, Creative Media and Entertainment: Sector Skills Assessment 2012 Briefing Paper. https://assets.publishing.service.gov.uk/government/uploads/system/uploads/attachment_data/file/306379/briefing-paper-ssa12-creative.pdf. Accessed 23 May 2023
21. The British Film Institute's Statistical Yearbook. https://core-cms.bfi.org.uk/media/24979/download. Accessed 23 May 2023
22. Gender Equality in UK TV Production. https://directors.uk.com/campaigns/gender-equality-in-uk-tv. Accessed 23 May 2023
23. Taylor, M.: UK Games Industry Census: Understanding diversity in the UK games industry workforce. https://ukie.org.uk/resources/uk-games-industry-census-2022. Accessed 23 May 2023
24. Hanan, A., Five facts that show how the advertising industry fails women. https://www.theguardian.com/women-in-leadership/2016/feb/03/how-advertising-industry-fails-women. Accessed 23 May 2023
25. DCMS Creative Industries: Focus on Employment. https://assets.publishing.service.gov.uk/government/uploads/system/uploads/attachment_data/file/534305/Focus_on_Employment_revised_040716.pdf. Accessed 23 May 2023
26. Mateos-Garcia, J., Bakshi,H.: The Geography of Creativity in the UK Creative clusters, creative people and creative networks. https://www.nesta.org.uk/documents/510/the_geography_of_creativity_in_the_uk.pdf. Accessed 23 May 2023
27. Swords, J., Wray, F.: The connectivity of the creative industries in North East England — the problems of physical and relational distance. Local Economy: The J. Local Econ. Policy Unit **25**(4), 305–318 (2010)

28. Women in Tech North East. https://www.youtube.com/@WomenInTechNE/about. Accessed 23 May 2023
29. Boldly Grow. https://thedigitalcity.com/services/cftv/boldlygrow/. Accessed 23 May 2023
30. Bowman, S.L.: Social Conflict in Role-Playing Communities: An Exploratory Qualitative Study, McFarland & Co, North Carolina, US (2010)
31. Bowman, S.L.: The Functions of Role-Playing Games: How Participants Create Community, Solve Problems and Explore Identity. Jefferson: McFarland & Co, North Carolina, US (2010)

Designing a Master Course Curriculum for Innovation Through Living Labs

Konstantinos G. Diamantis[1]([⊠]) [iD], Evdokimos I. Konstantinidis[1,2] [iD],
Teemu Santonen[3] [iD], Eva Kehayia[4] [iD], Despoina Petsani[1] [iD], Martina Desole[2],
Francesca Spagnoli[2], and Panagiotis D. Bamidis[1,2] [iD]

[1] Aristotle University of Thessaloniki, 54124 Thessaloniki, Greece
diamkons@auth.gr, evdokimosk@gmail.com, despoinapets@gmail.com,
pdbamidis@gmail.com
[2] European Network of Living Labs, Brussels, Belgium
{martina.desole, francesca.spagnoli}@enoll.org
[3] Laurea University of Applied Sciences, Espoo, Finland
teemu.santonen@laurea.fi
[4] McGill University, Montreal, QC, Canada
eva.kehayia@mcgill.ca

Abstract. Open innovation is increasingly important in today's world as it leverages access to diverse knowledge and expertise, enhances problem-solving, creativity, and market-driven innovation. Living Labs are open innovation ecosystems that have demonstrated potential towards supporting innovation through real-life interventions and multi-method approaches. The Living Lab approach, methodologies and tools for open innovation are complex and require diverse skills for successful implementation. Developing these skills and competencies within an organization is essential for effectively implementing open innovation strategies and maximizing the benefits it can bring. The presented methodology, followed during the VITALISE H2020 project, goes through the steps for identifying the key skills and content needed for effectively utilizing Living Labs in Open Innovation. The course methodology was designed, involving context analysis, identification of the learning skills and competencies, design of the course modules and the courses' lectures. It was found that there is a wide range of topics that should be included in such a master course, including the basics of Open Innovation, Living Lab research, stakeholder engagement, user-centred design and innovation management.

Keywords: Open Innovation · Living Labs · education course · curriculum · students

1 Introduction

1.1 Open Innovation and Living Labs

Open innovation is increasingly important in today's world as it leverages on access to diverse knowledge and expertise, enhanced problem-solving and creativity and market-driven innovation [1]. Open innovation methodologies provide frameworks and tools

D. Crawford et al. (Eds.): TIE 2023, LNICST 575, pp. 54–63, 2024.
https://doi.org/10.1007/978-3-031-59383-3_4

to facilitate the integration of external input into the innovation process [2]. Among the open innovation methodologies, crowdsourcing involves seeking ideas, solutions, or feedback from a large group of people, often through online platforms while open collaboration platforms provide a space for individuals or organizations to collaborate on innovation projects. They enable the sharing of ideas, knowledge, and resources, facilitating co-creation and problem-solving among participants. Following this, user co-creation, involving users or customers in the innovation process proved to lead to valuable insights and ideas [3]. Techniques such as user feedback, surveys, and user-centered design approaches can help capture user preferences and needs, driving innovation that aligns with customer expectations. To this end, it is obvious that the complexity of open innovation relies mainly in the skills required for collaboration and networking with a wide range of external stakeholders, facilitation of workshops and co-creation activities and cross-disciplinary knowledge management. These skills are essential for professionals from various fields for effectively implementing open innovation strategies and maximizing the benefits it can bring [4].

According to the definition of the European Network of Living Labs, a Living Lab is an innovative research and development ecosystem that provides a framework for the engagement of relevant stakeholders to co-create, test, and validate new products, services, or processes in a real-life setting [5]. It involves a collaborative approach that brings together researchers, entrepreneurs, public authorities, and citizens to design and implement solutions that provide value for the involved stakeholders and address complex social, economic, and environmental challenges. Living Labs aim to foster open innovation, user-centricity, and sustainability while providing a platform for experimentation and learning. Consequently, Living Labs can be used as a means to promote and effectively adopt open innovation principles in companies.

1.2 Open Innovation Educational Programs

The required skills and knowledge for Open Innovation management and application within an organization are diverse and complicated to acquire [6]. Some universities offer specialized master's programs in open innovation or related fields. These programs provide in-depth education on open innovation methodologies, strategies, and implementation. They typically cover topics such as collaboration, intellectual property management, technology transfer, and open innovation ecosystems [7]. Many universities offer programs that integrate open innovation concepts within broader innovation and entrepreneurship curricula. These programs aim to develop students' skills and knowledge in creating and managing innovative ventures, emphasizing the importance of collaboration and external inputs in the innovation process. Similarly, they organize workshops and seminars that bring together students, researchers, industry professionals, and experts to discuss open innovation trends, share case studies, and explore practical approaches to implementing open innovation [8]. In other cases, open innovation courses are often offered as part of business, management, or innovation-focused programs. These courses introduce students to the principles, methods, and tools of open innovation. They cover topics such as idea generation, crowdsourcing, collaboration strategies, and open innovation implementation in different industries. Universities may establish innovation hubs or centers that serve as platforms for open innovation education and research. These hubs provide spaces for interdisciplinary collaboration, facilitate industry-academia partnerships, and offer training programs, workshops, and events focused on open innovation [9]. Equally important, an increasing number of universities often collaborate with industry partners on open innovation initiatives. These collaborations can involve joint research projects, innovation challenges, or consulting engagements [10]. Finally, online learning platforms, such as Coursera, edX, and Udemy, offer open innovation courses and modules. These courses provide flexibility for students to learn at their own pace and are often developed by renowned universities or experts in the field of innovation.

The European Network of Living Labs already provides capacity building programs on how to build, sustain and govern a living lab (https://enoll.org/about-us/learning-lab). The capacity building program has been also recently expanding by providing trainings to researchers on how to utilize Living Lab methodologies in their research (https://vit alise-project.eu/vitalise-summer-school-2023/) as part of the VITALISE project. However, there is the need for post-graduate education programs on Open innovation by utilizing existing Living Lab infrastructures and methodologies. Such programs need to provide students with an understanding of the Living Lab methodologies, services and tools that can fit very well to the open innovation process. There are already some studies that evaluated the effectiveness of a Living Lab education program in promoting innovation in specific sectors, such as energy [11]. Furthermore, Living Labs have been also incorporated in higher education to support Research and Innovation in Ambient Intelligence [12].

1.3 Key Skillset and Content Needed for Open Innovation through LLs

According to the living lab principles, strong collaboration and communication skills are crucial for working effectively, including active listening, fostering a collaborative atmosphere, and effectively conveying ideas and insights to others. This skillset is fundamental for the ability to facilitate co-creation sessions and workshops towards driving innovation within a living lab. This involves guiding participants through ideation, problem-solving, and decision-making processes while ensuring everyone's input is valued and integrated. To do so, understanding and empathizing with users' needs and perspectives is vital for successful open innovation through living labs. Developing a user-centric mindset involves conducting user research, observing behavior, and incorporating user feedback to inform the innovation process. Other key skills include design thinking, an iterative problem-solving approach that emphasizes human-centered design helping in uncovering user insights, generating creative solutions, prototyping, and testing ideas within a living lab context. Consequently, engaging and managing stakeholders within a living lab environment is crucial. This includes building relationships, understanding stakeholders' motivations and expectations, and effectively involving them in the innovation process to ensure their perspectives are considered. In addition, living labs bring together individuals with diverse backgrounds and expertise. Being able to collaborate and integrate knowledge across disciplines is essential for leveraging the collective intelligence and generating innovative solutions within a living lab. The living lab methodologies generate vast amounts of data, including user feedback, sensor data, and other relevant information [13]. Proficiency in data analysis and interpretation enables extracting meaningful insights and trends from the data to inform decision-making and iterative improvement.

Closer to the open innovation important skills, as it is an iterative process, and being open to learning, adapting, and iterating based on feedback and insights is essential, the adaptive learning skill is of major importance. This includes a growth mindset, embracing failure as an opportunity to learn, and continuously improving and refining ideas and solutions. Finally, an entrepreneurial mindset embracing uncertainty, taking calculated risks, and being proactive in identifying and pursuing opportunities are an important skill. It enables individuals to think creatively, identify market potential, and drive the implementation and scaling of innovative solutions.

1.4 Goals and Objectives

Living Labs are becoming increasingly popular in open innovation research and education [14]. This paper aims to provide the methodology for designing an educational post-graduate program, targeting Open Innovation through Living Labs. The presented methodology, followed during the VITALISE H2020 project (https://vitalise-project.eu), goes through the steps of identifying the key skills and content needed to effectively utilise Living Labs.

2 Methods

The course design methodology was thoughtfully crafted and diligently executed to foster a comprehensive comprehension of the intricacies, challenges, and potential opportunities inherent in the practical application of open innovation within the realm of Living Labs. In addition to the extensive literature review, surveys, discussions with key partners and ethnographic methods were utilized to successfully capture the dynamics of open innovation in action and the use of Living Lab principles on that direction [15]. This involved observing and interviewing stakeholders and focusing on their experiences to elicit insights that would drive the curriculum design.

2.1 Methodology for Curriculum Design and Development

The collaborative efforts of curriculum designers, educators, and stakeholders were guided by a shared vision of creating a dynamic and forward-looking learning experience [16]. The curriculum design methodology not only focused on needs analysis and assessment but also placed a strong emphasis on cultivating an open innovation mindset among students. This involved incorporating design thinking methodologies, experiential learning opportunities within the Living Lab context [8], and interdisciplinary collaboration to foster creativity, problem-solving skills, and entrepreneurial thinking. By intertwining the principles of innovation with curriculum design, this methodology aimed to equip students with the mindset and skills required to drive meaningful change in the real world. The main steps followed during the curriculum design were the context analysis, the identification of the learning skills and competencies, the design of the course modules and the courses' lectures design.

Context Analysis

The first phase of the model starts with analysing the context in which the curriculum is developed. The analysis of the situation includes a study of the different curriculum sources (students, stakeholders and disciplines or subject matter), and careful examination of the different curriculum influences (internal, external, and organizational) that affect curriculum development. Following the selected methodology, and by involving a number of experts, professors and students, a gap in the postgraduate curricula was identified. The target group of students that the MSc aims at will consist of various disciplines (e.g., doctors, engineers, psychologists, innovation managers). The proposed course will focus on innovation through Living Labs methodologies, services and entrepreneurship.

The proposed master course is determined by the following basic characteristics.

- Aims to create an innovative and pioneering postgraduate program of study which will combine the philosophy and culture developed by the LLs with the creation of innovation within a business development framework
- Aims to provide educational as well as business content
- It has specific learning and educational goals with time, financial and quality limitations
- During its implementation it will utilize human and material resources.

Course Modules and Learning Skills

This step includes the development of the goals and objectives of the curriculum as well as the learning skills and competencies. In this phase the thematic areas were decided and the expected skills per area were identified. A core group of experts in courses designing, innovation management and living lab methodology was formed from members of the VITALISE consortium. After concluding the target objective of the course and the target users, the identification of the learning skills and competencies took place. A set of initial learning skills led to the creation of the teaching modules (groups of skills belonging to the same concept). To make this process more effective, "Cards-Lectures", cards containing the learning skills and describing what each skill is, were designed and used. The usage of the cards facilitated the core group to identify the modules during an in-person meeting. Then, after discussions among the members of the core group, more learning skills were added to the corresponding teaching modules. In addition, initial ideas on hands on assignments, tools and methods for collaboration among the students and expected studying outcomes were also included. The first version of the course was composed of 13 course teaching modules and ~7 learning skills each.

Lectures Design

The next step, towards designing the lectures, was to estimate the time/effort each teaching skill would require to be taught. To do so, the Planning Poker approach was borrowed by the Scrum framework [17]. Planning Poker is a consensus based, gamified technique to estimate the complexity and effort needed. Planning Poker depends upon input from all the experts with their different fields of expertise who are actively involved. In planning poker, members of the group make estimates by playing numbered cards face-down to the table, instead of speaking them aloud. The cards are revealed, and the estimates are then discussed. Before starting this, the members were invited to select 1–2 learning skills that would require a 2-h lecture to be taught. The commonly selected lectures were used as a reference of a lecture's duration.

Taking into account the estimated duration of each learning skill and the teaching module, the learning skills were group to form full 2-h lectures. Given the short duration of some lectures, and after reflecting on the result, the core team decided to combine similar topics.

Teaching Model

The course development methodology embraces the concept of innovation by using the 5E teaching model and incorporating dynamic elements within each phase. In the engagement phase, teachers not only tap into students' prior knowledge but also encourage them to think innovatively by asking open-ended questions that stimulate curiosity and encourage diverse perspectives [18].

During the exploration phase, the methodology encourages students to actively engage in questioning, investigation, and hands-on activities [19]. This emphasis on experiential learning within the Living Labs environment fosters a culture of innovation. Teachers play a crucial role as facilitators, guiding students to think critically, experiment, and make connections between concepts. The collaborative and open learning environment encourages the exchange of ideas and the exploration of innovative solutions to real-world challenges.

The explanation phase of the methodology provides a platform for students to express their observations and findings in their own words, fostering their ability to articulate innovative ideas. Teachers play a supportive role by providing explanations and definitions, bridging the gap between informal and formal language. This stage encourages students to think creatively and develop novel approaches to problem-solving, thereby enhancing their capacity for innovation.

In the elaboration phase, students are encouraged to apply their newly acquired knowledge to novel or similar situations, promoting innovative thinking and solution generation. Teachers support this process by building on previously learned information, creating opportunities for students to extend their understanding and explore innovative applications [20]. The emphasis is not only on solving problems but also on encouraging students to think innovatively, push boundaries, and develop unique perspectives.

The evaluation phase of the methodology incorporates elements that promote critical thinking and reflection, essential components of innovation. Students are assessed through self-, peer-, and teacher-assessment, which encourages them to analyze their understanding, reflect on their learning journey, and identify areas for improvement. Open-ended questions and discussions stimulate students' higher order thinking skills, enabling them to evaluate concepts and propose innovative approaches. The integration of a variety of tools and technologies, such as Padlet, Google Classroom Question, Zoom, and Google Forms, can enrich the assessment process and encourage innovative ways of assessing students' knowledge and skills.

3   Results

The first version of the course was composed of 13-course teaching modules. The titles of the course teaching modules along with the key skills to be learnt are presented in Table 1:

Table 1. Course module names and key skills

No.	Course module name	Key skills to be learnt
1	Course introduction and orientation	Understanding the course objectives and committing to forthcoming studying tasks
2	Theoretical foundation of user centric methods and innovation	Understanding the theoretical foundations and becoming familiar with the current body of knowledge regarding user centric innovation
3	Innovation typology	Understanding different innovation types and their relation to user centric innovation methods
4	Stakeholder identification	Understanding and classification of different user types and the different contexts they operate in
5	Needs assessment and problem definition	Ability to identify user needs, scope the problem and find the opportunity for innovation. Understanding better the problem to be solved
6	Survey, interview and focus group methodologies in user centric research	Ability to conduct survey, interview and focus group methods
7	Co-creation sessions Ideation, conceptualization and prototyping techniques	Ability to understand and use co-creation techniques for ideating, concept creation and prototyping. Recognise the potential of co-creation
8	Testing experimentation and validation techniques	Understanding different types of testing methods. Ability to formulate testing plan and conduct testing for different types of tests
9	Research ethics and legal issues. Data management and protection	Ability to execute living lab research in ethical way and follow GDPR and other national/international regulation requirements. Ability to create data management plan and foster open data principles

(continued)

Table 1. (*continued*)

No.	Course module name	Key skills to be learnt
10	User / research panel management	Theoretical foundations of user/research panel management
11	Living lab project planning and management	Ability to define project plan for a living lab project
12	Entrepreneurship	Collaborate effectively with your team in Living Labs to generate innovative ideas and foster entrepreneurship
13	Sustainability	How the co-creation of knowledge and practices takes place within LLs to address sustainability challenges

4 Discussion

The study aimed to present the methodology followed for designing a Master course curriculum for Innovation through Living Labs. A multi-method approach combining literature review, surveys, and partner discussions was used. By synthesizing insights from diverse sources, the study's results shed light on the main course modules and key skills to be imparted in the Master Course. It was found that there is a wide range of topics, including the basics of Open Innovation, Living Lab research, stakeholder engagement, user-centred design and innovation management. In addition, the results also showed that there is an overlap between the different topics, in particular in the areas of user-centred design and innovation management, both of which are central to Open Innovation and Living Lab research. These overlaps highlight the need for clarification and standardisation of course content in order to create a robust and well-structured Innovation through Living Labs education program. The study's outcomes hold the potential to offer valuable insights and recommendations to educators involved in Innovation training. By providing a detailed methodology and essential tools for innovation through the lens of Living Labs, the study equips educators with the means to cultivate a transformative learning experience. Building upon the existing body of knowledge, the study enriches the understanding of designing effective curricula for Innovation through Living Labs, bridging the gap between theory and practice.

4.1 Practical Implications

The study has significant practical implications. The current study designed the courses and set the structure for the lectures. The next steps are to produce the lecture contents, the assignments for each of the lectures and to design and run a small-scale pilot of the master program. The pilot will be executed collaboratively among three universities: Aristotle University of Thessaloniki, Laurea University and McGill university. The master course was designed for a 3-semesters program. However, the small-scale pilot will be conducted as 1 semester course, especially due to the limitations of the VITALISE

H2020 project. Further evaluation of the Master course is needed in order to establish the education of Open innovation through Living Labs.

Acknowledgement. This research was funded by the VITALISE (Virtual Health and Wellbeing LivingLab Infrastructure) project, funded by the Horizon 2020 Framework Program of the European Union for Research Innovation (grant agreement 101007990).

References

1. Huizingh, E.K.R.E.: Open innovation: State of the art and future perspectives. Technovation **31**(1) (2011). https://doi.org/10.1016/j.technovation.2010.10.002
2. Gascó, M.: Living labs: Implementing open innovation in the public sector. Gov. Inf. Q. **34**(1), 90–98 (2017). https://doi.org/10.1016/j.giq.2016.09.003
3. Schuurman, D., Ballon, P., Van Hoed, M.: The effectiveness of involving users in digital innovation: Measuring the impact of living labs (2018). https://doi.org/10.1016/j.tele.2018.02.003
4. Kratzer, J., Meissner, D., Roud, V.: Open innovation and company culture: Internal openness makes the difference. Technol. Forecast Soc. Change, 119 (2017). https://doi.org/10.1016/j.techfore.2017.03.022
5. Vervoort, K., et al.: Harmonizing the evaluation of living labs: a standardised evaluation framework. In: ISPIM Innovation Conference 2022 (2022). https://doi.org/10.5281/zenodo.7434406
6. Leminen, S., Westerlund, M., Nyström, A.-G.: Living labs as open-innovation networks. Technol. Innov. Manag. Rev. **2**(9), 6–11 (2012). https://doi.org/10.22215/timreview/602
7. Iglesias-Sánchez, P.P., Jambrino-Maldonado, C., de las Heras-Pedrosa, C.: Training entrepreneurial competences with open innovation paradigm in higher education. Sustainability (Switzerland), vol. 11, no. 17 (2019). https://doi.org/10.3390/su11174689
8. Konstantinidis, E.I., Petsani, D., Bamidis, P.D.: Teaching university students co-creation and living lab methodologies through experiential learning activities and preparing them for RRI. Health Informatics J. **27**(1), 146045822199120 (2021). https://doi.org/10.1177/146045822 1991204
9. Konstantinidis, E.I., Billis, A., Bratsas, C., Siountas, A., Bamidis, P.D.: Thessaloniki active and healthy ageing living lab: the roadmap from a specific project to a living lab towards openness. In: ACM International Conference Proceeding Series (2016). doi: https://doi.org/10.1145/2910674.2935846
10. Santonen, T., Kjellson, F., Andersson, K., Hirvikoski, T.: Developing maturity model for transnational living lab collaboration. In: Proceedings of the 2020 ISPIM Innovation Conference (Virtual) Event "Innovating in Times of Crisis" held on 7 to 10 June 2020 (2020)
11. Mbatha, S.P., Musango, J.K.: A systematic review on the application of the living lab concept and role of stakeholders in the energy sector. Sustainability **14**(21), 14009 (2022). https://doi.org/10.3390/su142114009
12. Kröse, B., Veenstra, M., Robben, S., Kanis, M.: Living labs as educational tool for ambient intelligence. Lecture Notes in Computer Science (including subseries Lecture Notes in Artificial Intelligence and Lecture Notes in Bioinformatics) (2012). https://doi.org/10.1007/978-3-642-34898-3_27
13. Følstad, A.: Living labs for innovation and development of information and communication technology: a literature review. Electronic Journal for Virtual Organizations and Networks

14. Schuurman, D., Herregodts, A.-L., Georges, A., Rits, O.: Innovation management in living lab projects: the innovatrix framework. Technol. Innov. Manag. Rev. **9**(3), 63–73 (2019). https://doi.org/10.22215/timreview/1225

15. Kali, Y., McKenney, S., Sagy, O.: Teachers as designers of technology enhanced learning. Instr. Sci. **43**(2), 173–179 (2015). https://doi.org/10.1007/s11251-014-9343-4

16. Dekker, R., Franco Contreras, J., Meijer, A.: The living lab as a methodology for public administration research: a systematic literature review of its applications in the social sciences. Int. J. Public Administration **43**(14), 1207–1217 (2020). https://doi.org/10.1080/01900692.2019.1668410

17. Dalton, J.: Planning poker. Great Big Agile (2019). https://doi.org/10.1007/978-1-4842-4206-3_44

18. Rodriguez, S., Allen, K., Harron, J., Qadri, S.A.: Making and the 5E learning cycle. Sci. Teacher **86**(5), 48–55 (2019). https://www.jstor.org/stable/26899115

19. Wilson, C.D., Taylor, J.A., Kowalski, S.M., Carlson, J.: The relative effects and equity of inquiry-based and commonplace science teaching on students' knowledge, reasoning, and argumentation. J. Res. Sci. Teach, p. n/a-n/a (2009). https://doi.org/10.1002/tea.20329

20. Lam, A.H.C., Ho, K.K.W., Chiu, D.K.W.: Instagram for student learning and library promotions: a quantitative study using the 5E Instructional Model. Aslib J. Inf. Manag.Manag. **75**(1), 112–130 (2023). https://doi.org/10.1108/AJIM-12-2021-0389

Immersive Virtual Reality, Augmented Reality and Mixed Reality for Self-regulated Learning: A Review

Daniela Pedrosa[1,2](✉) 🆔 and Leonel Morgado[3] 🆔

[1] Higher School of Education, Polytechnic University of Santarém, Santarém, Portugal
dpedrosa@ua.pt
[2] Department of Education and Psychology, Universidade de Aveiro & Laboratory of Didactics of Science and Technology, Research Centre on Didactics and Technology in the Education of Trainers (CIDTFF), Aveiro, Portugal
[3] Universidade Aberta & INESC TEC, Coimbra, Portugal

Abstract. Immersive technologies, such as virtual reality, augmented reality, and mixed reality have gained increasing interest and usage in the field of education. Attention is being paid to their effects on teaching and learning processes, one of which is self-regulation of learning, with an important role in supporting learning success. However, designing and creating immersive environments that support the development of SRL strategies is challenging. Employing a systematic approach, this literature review provides an overview of the uses of virtual, augmented, and mixed reality with the goal of supporting SRL. We map these to known educational uses of immersive environments, highlighting current gaps in these efforts and suggesting pathways for future studies on instructional design of the use of immersive technologies to support self-regulation of learning.

Keywords: Self-regulated Learning · Immersive Environments · Immersive Learning · Virtual Reality · Augmented Reality · Mixed Reality

1 Introduction

There is an increasing use of immersive technologies (ImT) [1–9] for education and to their effects on teaching and learning processes [10]. Common examples are X-Reality technologies: augmented reality (AR), virtual reality (VR), and mixed reality (MR), spanning the physical and the virtual, allowing users to experience immersion [2, 4].

ImT create experiences in immersive learning environments (ILE) that are influenced by several factors: interactivity, personal variables, and self-regulated learning (SRL) [6, 11]. Their adoption requires assessment along students' cognitive, affective [1, 3], metacognitive and physiological dimensions [10, 12]. Clear strategies are also needed for instructors to select and implement them effectively in learning process [10]. For example, VR can be used to support instructional design and create opportunities

D. Crawford et al. (Eds.): TIE 2023, LNICST 575, pp. 64–81, 2024.
https://doi.org/10.1007/978-3-031-59383-3_5

to teach and learn, but it's *"necessary to construct "know-how" on effective VR applications for teaching and learning"* [7]. AR may be used to facilitate the *"development of processing skills"* [13], improve learning experiences, acquire significant knowledge and for motivation [8], but presents some issues: technological, management, and cognitive [8, 9, 13], and is necessary to understand how uses of AR contribute to effective teaching [13].

VR, AR, MR can contribute to SRL [6], stimulating social presence and reflection through meaningful interactions [6, 14]. However, these environments are cognitively demanding, which affects opportunities for reflection [15] and consequently may impair SRL, since students may have difficulty monitoring activation of their motivational, cognitive and metacognitive processes [11]. So, studies on uses and integration of immersive experiences for SRL [6, 16], testing and implementing SRL scenarios [16], and instructional design suited to educational goals [17] are essential.

This literature review mapped and described the uses of VR, AR, and MR explicitly to support SRL to support instructors in applying them to their contexts and highlight current research gaps.

2   Background

2.1   Self-regulation of Learning and Immersive Learning

Self-regulated learning (SRL) is a complex process [18]: a meta-process in which students actively participate for their regulation and control of emotional, behavioural, cognitive, metacognitive, cognitive, and environmental processes [19–21]. It involves adoption of SRL strategies: self-evaluation; organizing, transforming; goal setting; planning; seeking information; keeping records; monitoring; physical and psychological environmental structuring; self-consequences; review; memorization; seeking social assistance and reviewing records [19, 21].

SRL requires skills for selection and adoption of those strategies to achieve the learning goals and development of self-awareness, self-knowledge, self-assessment, and self-efficacy [19, 20, 22]. SRL allows developing independent learners who care about what to learn and how to learn it [23], that construct their meanings, define goals and adopt strategies based on the information available in the physical and psychological environment [18].

In parallel learning environments that can leverage the phenomenon of immersion [24], a psychological deep state of mental absorption that impacts affective and cognitive processes [25–27]. The phenomenon of Immersion, arises from three conceptual dimensions [25, 27]:

1) Agency – immersion occurs when we are actively engaged in tasks that require our cognitive and physical effort (also referred to as "challenge").
2) Narrative – immersion occurs when we are focused on the story and meaning of the elements that make up the moment (characters, plot, objects, space-time contexts, sounds, images and symbols, emotional attachment, etc.).
3) System – immersion stems from the feeling of being present in an environment, be it technological, physical, social, or organizational.

These dimensions are affected by technology and other mediating elements, and experienced in immersive learning environments (ILE) where different types of immersive technology (ImT) may be employed [27].

2.2 Immersive Technologies – VR, AR and MR

To understand what we mean by ImT, we proceed by leveraging the conceptualization of the virtuality-reality continuum proposed by Milgram and Kishino [5, 28, 29], considering it as extending between the physical and virtual worlds [30]. The physical environment is positioned on the far left of the continuum and is fully realized in tangible things. The virtual environment is on the far side and is made entirely of intangible objects [5, 29]. Between these extremes, we find mixed reality (MR), considered as an umbrella term for environments that combine virtual and physical elements [29]. Among these, Augmented Reality (AR) is centrally positioned to refer to those closer to the physical world, and Augmented Virtuality (AV) to refer to those closer to a virtual environment [2, 30]. Different forms of physicality [4] and virtuality can be found along the continuum [2].

Updated versions of Milgram and Kishino's proposal have emerged since, suggesting that MR may be a very specific type of reality that lies between AR and AV [31, 32]. Skarbez et al. [33] propose that MR is an environment in which physical and virtual objects are presented together in a single perception: the user simultaneously understands the physical and virtual content in different senses. These authors agree with the original definition of AR, however, considering that external VR is also a subset of MR, since the user can perceive virtual and physical content with different types of senses (introspection). They consider that VR only occurs when all the senses - exteroceptive and interoceptive - are completely altered by virtual contents. In this sense, VR can be achieved by using computing technologies to create and simulate realistic experiences in a virtual environment [7]. It gives the user the illusion of being involved ("sense of presence") in a 360° simulated three-dimensional (3D) environment with which they can explore and interact freely and with visual objects and elements created by computer graphics [4, 7]. In VR, the user immerses totally in a virtual environment [8, 10, 12, 28, 32] "without seeing the real world" [30] and lives immersive experiences with interactions and manipulations in virtual environment [1, 4, 10].

VR includes experimental tasks through computing devices such as head-mounted displays, and natural user interfaces, like body sensors (touch, voice, gestures) [7, 12], when the "*user has a headset that generates images and sounds similar to a real or imaginary world*" [10]. It can be categorized into 4 forms of interaction: 1) Cave Automatic Virtual Environments (CAVEs) – room-sized displays involving the users; 2) Head-mounted displays (HMDs); 3) Mobile VR with portable monitors (tablets) and smartphones; and 4) wearable 360° spherical video-based VR [2, 7].

AR can be seen as a technology to create immersive hybrid learning environments that overlays virtual objects (augmented components) with physical, tangible objects, coexisting in the same space and time [1, 2, 4, 8, 9, 12, 13, 28, 30, 32]. AR is a mix between virtuality and physicality [5, 8, 28, 30], and requires triggers "*to activate a boost (a 3D material overlay)*" as "*marker-based, marker less, image-based, positional and locational AR*" [28], using the movement of a user's mobile device to display the mix environments [2, 5]. AR can be used through different technologies, such as desktop computers, HMDs, 3D glasses, tablet PCs, or popular mobile devices [9, 10]. These allow the live visualization of the physical world with integration of virtual information elements, such as sound, video, images, or GPS data [4, 10]. AR can also enhance or replace senses such as smell, touch, and audition [30], using specialized hardware, e.g.: depth sensors, eye tracking, retinal displays, and also leverage somatic human-computer interfaces: controllers, hand and finger tracking, and other interfaces such as voice commands, retinal control, or brain-computer interfaces [32].

MR, sometimes also called hybrid/extended reality, is understood as the shared inter-action of experiences between the real and virtual environment [28], with physical and digital objectives coexisting mentally in real time [2, 5, 10, 12], across the entire virtual-reality continuum [28], and pursuing them with manipulation of virtual objects in the context of the physical world [4, 28, 34], in different ways [3]. The difference between MR and AR is the capacity to seamlessly interact between virtual overlays and the physical world [3, 28, 35].

3   Methodology

3.1   Planning: Purpose, Goals, and Research Question

We adopted the systematic literature review method proposed by Kitchenham and her colleagues [36]. The focus of this work was to provide an overview of uses of AR, VR, MR to support SRL.

The research question was "What is the panorama of uses of AR, VR, MR for developing SRL?" The specific goals were thus defined as:

1) Identify studies in which ImT (AR, VR, MR) are used to support SRL, in terms of
   a) Year of publication; b) Study field; c) Pedagogical context; d) Research Design; e) Research Sample; f) Duration of study; g) Research Instruments.
2) Identify and describe the uses of ImT to support SRL found in those studies and map them to the conceptual space of immersion.

3.2   Review Process

This review took place in October 2022, explicitly for the terms "self-regulation of learning" and "immersion". The process was organized in five phases (Fig. 1).

Phase 1 - Literature Search. Search for relevant literature on bibliographic databases: SCOPUS, WoS, ACM, and ERIC, with the search string: ("Self-Regulated learning" OR "Self-Regulation of Learning") AND ("Immersion" OR "Immersive"). We did not delimit by publication date and only considered peer-reviewed papers in these languages: English, Portuguese, or Spanish. We found 92 papers as potentially relevant (SCOPUS, n = 31; WoS, n = 22; ERIC, n = 6; ACM, n = 33).

Phase 2 - Screening for Inclusion. The 92 papers were screened for inclusion. In a first screen, we analysed titles and abstracts with these inclusion criteria: a) explicitly incor-porating the search terms in the abstract: "self-regulated learning" or "self-regulation learning", and "immersion" or "immersive"; b) written in these languages: English, Portuguese, or Spanish; c) all educational contexts and research designs were included. We removed papers that we could not access or found to be duplicated. This excluded 66 papers: a) 27 without both term options; b) 16 without full text; c) 8 papers we could not access, and d) 16 duplicates. This results in 25 papers.

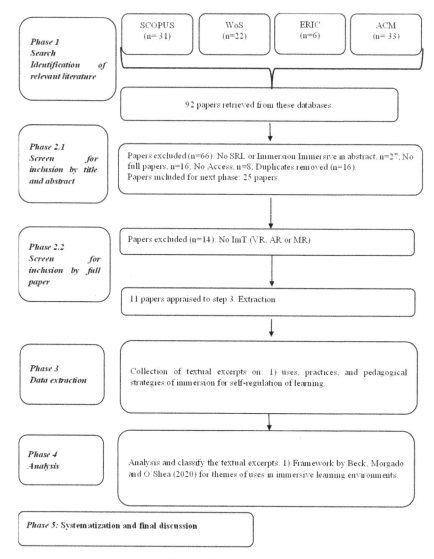

Fig. 1. Work process.

In a second screen, we analysed paper contents entirely, with the inclusion criterium: a) reporting uses of ImT to support SRL. This eliminated 14 papers that did not use these technologies, resulting in 11 papers of review corpus (see Table 1).

Table 1. Corpus of final papers.

ID	Authors	Year	Title
P1	Rahayu & Jacobson	2012	Speaking self-efficacy and English as a foreign language: learning processes in a multi-user
P2	Sakdavong et al.	2019	Virtual Reality in Self-regulated Learning: Example in Art Domain
P3	Chen & Hsu	2020	Self-regulated mobile game-based English learning in a virtual reality environment
P4	Nachtigall et al.	2022	Fostering cognitive strategies for learning with 360° videos in history education contexts
P5	Spiliotopoulos et al.	2019	A Mixed-reality Interaction-driven Game-based Learning Framework
P6	Boomgaard et al.	2022	A Novel Immersive Anatomy Education System (Anat_Hub): Redefining Blended Learning for the Musculoskeletal System
P7	Hayashida et al.	2020	Virtually Alone-How Facilitated Aloneness Affect Self-Study in IVE
P8	Li	2017	Design of Multimedia Teaching Platform for Chinese Folk Art Performance Based on Virtual Reality Technology
P9	Nietfeld et al.	2014	Self-Regulation and Gender Within a Game-Based Learning Environment
P10	Cheng & Tsai	2020	Students' motivational beliefs and strategies, perceived immersion and attitudes towards science learning with immersive virtual reality: A partial least squares analysis
P11	Perera & Allison	2015	Self-Regulated Learning in Virtual Worlds – An Exploratory Study in OpenSim

Phase 3 – Extraction. We collected data by extracting text excerpts from the paper corpus, regarding these aspects:

1) Characterization of the sample (papers) in terms of a) year of publication; b) Study field; c) pedagogical context; d) Research Design; e) Research Sample; f) Duration of study; g) Research Instruments.
2) Descriptions of uses of ImT for SRL (56 text excerpts were extracted).

Phase 4 – Analysis. We conducted descriptive statistical analysis of the studies (goal 1). Regarding the descriptions of uses of VR, AR, or MR (goal 2), we performed thematic content analysis [37], to identify relevant themes. We then employed Beck et al.'s framework to map them to the immersion conceptual space and compare them to overall known uses of ILE [27]. Afterwards, we conducted descriptive statistical analysis to identify their prevalence. Subsequently, a summary was carried out on how each study/paper used ImT for SRL, to illustrate the identified themes.

Phase 5 - Systematization and Final Discussion of Results. We present in the next section the results and discuss about the panorama of uses the ImT to support SRL, and provide recommendations for further work.

4 Results and Discussion

4.1 Characterization of Studies About the Uses of VR, AR, MR for SRL

Years of Publication. Of the 11 papers, studies on VR, AR and MR for SRL are recent: the first paper is from 2012, and interest increased only in the latest 5 years (n = 7) (Fig. 2).

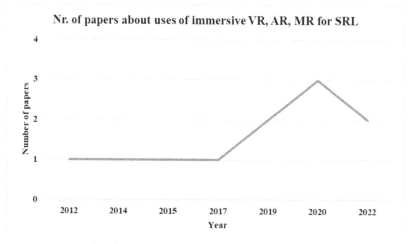

Fig. 2. Evolution of papers about ImT for SRL.

Study Fields. There is variability (Language; Art; Technology; General; Medicine; Biology; History; Social Sciences), with none having a significantly higher prevalence (Fig. 3).

Educational Context. Higher education is predominant (n = 6), with mentions of Basic Education (n = 3), Secondary Education (n = 1), Unspecified (n = 1). There were no studies for preschool education (Fig. 4).

Although the sample of studies is small (n = 11), it demonstrates that the interest in using these technologies to support SRL is increasing, that they are used in various fields, and particularly in Higher Education. Other teaching contexts are fields that deserve to be explored.

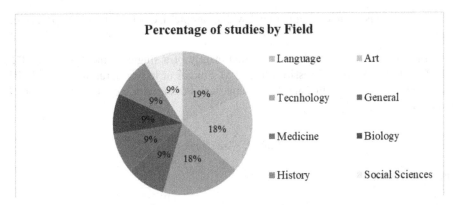

Fig. 3. Study fields.

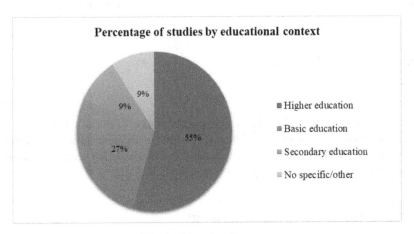

Fig. 4. Educational context.

Research Design. There is a tendency towards experimental or quasi-experimental studies (see Table 2), predominantly using quantitative methods for data analysis.

Table 2. Research design.

Type	Nr. of papers	ID
Experimental	5	P2; P7; P8; P9; P10
Quasi-experimental	2	P3; P4
Case Study	1	P11
Mixed	1	P1
Pilot Study - Participatory design	1	P6
Interactive design	1	P5

Sample. There is a tendency for studies with a sample size below 100 participants (see Table 3).

Duration of Study. The studies are predominantly of a single moment, e.g.: P1; P2; P4; P7; P9; P10; P11; or 2 sessions (e.g., P5). Studies of longer duration were only P3 with a duration of 2 months, and P8 (1 semester). P6 does not mention the duration of intervention.

Table 3. Size sample.

Research Sample	Nr. of papers	ID
<10	1	P1
11 to 50	2	P5; P7
51 to 100	5	P2; P6; P8; P10; P11
101 to 150	1	P9
151 to 200	1	P4
>200	1	P3

Research Instruments for SRL. There is a predominance of quantitative instruments, such as questionnaires and surveys. The dispersion of instruments used is evident, with no common instruments among the studies, which may indicate the need for comparable instruments to evaluate/measure SRL in concert with ImT (Table 4).

4.2   Uses of Immersive VR, AR, MR for SRL

Table 5 shows how the 56 accounts were associated with 18 themes, identifying uses of ImT for SRL [27, 38]. These match 12 of the 16 themes found in Beck et al.'s framework of uses of ILE, and also 1 theme reported in a previous study [38]. Five themes have no matching to previous studies.

In more than half of the papers (n = 7; 63.6%), we found the most prevalent use: *"Interactive manipulation and exploration"*, and the same happens in terms of text extracts extracted (17.9%). This use combines these immersion dimensions: High agency and High system. Samples:

> *"(…) familiarization was intended to train the participant, during ten minutes, to use the material and its resources."* Text excerpt from P9.

> *"The students may interactively explore other trees and scenery, trigger wind and rain."* Text excerpt from P5.

The use *"Skill Training"* is the second most prevalent theme, found in almost half of the papers (n = 5, 45.5%) and in 16.1% of the excerpts. It is associated with these immersion dimensions: High agency and Mid-Narrative. Samples:

Table 4. Research instruments for SRL.

Research Instruments for SRL	ID
Questionnaire adapted from Wang (2004) to measure self-efficacy	P1
Interviews about learning habits	P1
Participant observation (DeWalt et al., 98) focused on behaviour & learning process	P1
Questionnaire adapted from Wang (2004) to measure self-efficacy	P1
Adapted questionnaire integrating 2 indicators (time management and metacognition) from Pintrich (2000) and 1 (emotional perception) from Deci et al. (1994)	P2
Game Engagement Questionnaire (GEQ) from Brockmyer et al.'s (2009)	P3
Motivated Strategies for Learning Questionnaire (MSLQ) adapted from Pintrich	P3; P10
Strategy use test (pre- and post-test) on students' cognitive strategies knowledge	P4
Mock-ups to support reflection	P5
Discuss in group	P5
Survey	P6; P8
SDT to measure of intrinsic motivation	P7
Intrinsic Motivation Inventory (IMI)	P7
Measures of cognitive abilities (knowledge and strategy use), self-reported beliefs, trace logs, and measures of calibration	P9
Achievement Goals Questionnaire (AGQ) Scale	P9
Science Learning Self-Efficacy Inventory	P9
Perceived Interest Questionnaire (PIQ)	P9
In-game performance	P9
Immersive Experience Questionnaire (IEQ) from Jennett et al. (2008)	P10
Attitudes survey from Cheng's (2017)	P10
Questionnaire	P11

"SRL training that fostered students' acquisition of cognitive strategies for processing history-related 360° videos (…)" Text excerpt from P4.

"(…) [Crystal Island-Outbreak] students are aware of the overall goal and must successfully navigate through a number of subgoals (…)" Text excerpt from P9.

The uses *"Engagement"* and *"Complement/Combine contexts, media, or items"* also appear in almost half of the analysed papers (45.5%), but with a lower prevalence than previously mentioned themes, with 12,9% and 8.9% respectively. Engagement focuses on high agency immersion, and Complement/Combine in high system immersion. Samples:

Table 5. Uses of VR, AR, and MR for SRL.

Use of ILE	Nr. of papers (n = 11)	Nr. of excerpts (n = 56)	ID papers
Interactive manipulation and exploration	7 (63.6%)	10 (17.9%)	P2 (x2); P3; P5 (x2); P7; P9; P10; P11(x2)
Skill training	5 (45.5%)	9 (16.1%)	P1; P4 (x4); P5; P6; P21 (x2)
Engagement	5 (45.5%)	7 (12.5%)	P1; P3; P5 (x2); P9 (x2); P11
Complement/Combine contexts, media, or items	5 (45.5%)	5 (8.9%)	P4; P5; P6; P10; P11
Collaboration	4 (36.4%)	6 (10.7%)	P1; P4; P5(x3); P10
Simulate the physical world	3 (27.3%)	4 (7.1%)	P1; P2; P3 (x2)
Mobile Learning	2 (18.2%)	4 (7.1%)	P3 (x3); P5
Augmented context	2 (18.2%)	3 (5.4%)	P5 (x2); P10;
Changing human behaviour	2 (18.2%)	2 (3.6%)	P4; P10
Perspective switching	2 (18.2%)	2 (3.6%)	P7; P11
Multimodal interaction	2 (18.2%)	2 (3.6%)	P3; P7
Data collection	1 (9.1%)	1 (1.8%)	P5
Emotional and cultural experiences	1 (9.1%)	1 (1.8%)	P8
LMS	0	0	-
Emphasis	0	0	-
Logistics	0	0	-
Accessibility	0	0	-
Seeing the invisible	0	0	-

"The learning environment (...) showing remaining learning items (progress), hinting or providing gamification-driven bonus feedback to students that explore." Text excerpt from P5 (engagement theme).

"Wireless Island (...) a dedicated region for wireless communication education, (...) lecture notes, lecture media streams and a museum of the history of wireless communication (...)" Text excerpt from P11 (complement theme).

The use *"Collaboration"* also has some prevalence, found in 4 papers (36.4%) and in 10,7% of text excerpts. It is also associated with high agency immersion. Sample:

"(...) design of collaborative inquiry-based tasks (...)." Text excerpt from P10.

"students (...) share newfound information that they believe that may be of interest to the rest of the learners, and later discuss their rationale on how they chose to learn (paths, logical, deductions, completeness, experience, etc.)." Text excerpt from P15.

Some use themes appear with residual prevalence (7.1% to 1.8%):

Simulate the physical world, e.g.: *"(...) participants attended a class in Second Life with a person's avatar as the teacher (...)"* Text excerpt from P1.

Mobile Learning, for example: *"(...) assigned to study English using a newly created mobile learning app (...)"* Text excerpt from P3.

Augmented context, e.g.: *"(...) adopted the application (app) (...) allows a teacher using a tablet PC (or a smartphone) to broadcast 360° spherical image-based content (...) to his or her students' VR headsets with smartphones."* Text excerpt from P22.

Changing human behaviour, for example: *"(...) fostering students' scientific intrinsic values when learning science with the aid of IVR."* Text excerpt from P10.

Perspective switching, for example: *"Learning aids and content objects in a MUVE are put in-world with specific positions; if students change the terrain shape and land height it can completely change the intended learning experience."* Text excerpt from P11.

Multimodal interaction, e.g.: *"Even though the displayed text changed automatically after every pre-determined time slot, natural use included taking short breaks at any point between task beginning and task end (...)"* Text excerpt from P7.

Data collection, e.g.: *"(...) interaction feedback can be logged and analysed to assess the young users' expectations of the technology (...)"* Text excerpt from P5.

And finally, the use for Emotional and cultural experiences, for example: *"(...) VR-based Chinese folk-art performance (...) was implemented (...) realize interactive learning."* Text excerpt from P8.

Considering the reference framework by Beck et al., some themes were not found identified in the corpus papers, namely: accessibility, logistics, seeing the invisible. These are uses that combine high narrative immersion with significant amounts of system and agency immersion. Thus, we conclude that current uses of ImT to support SRL is leveraging only two of the dimensions of the immersion phenomenon: system-based and challenge-based immersion (see Fig. 5).

Table 6, shows there is a predominant use of VR (n = 6) to support the focus on system immersion, followed by MR (n = 4), AR having less prevalence (n = 1). From the uses of VR, AR, and MR, it appears that the support for the development of SRL is not very explicit and there is little concrete on how learning tasks were designed for students to apply/develop SRL strategies during the planning, execution, and evaluation tasks.

These results confirm that there is a need for further exploration, integration, testing, and creation of instructional design guidelines for immersive experiences in support of SRL [6, 16, 17].

One possible cause for this situation is that the corpus studies are mostly outcome-based experimental, seeking to understanding how such environments affect learning. This tendency towards experimental, quantitative, and applied studies in a single moment, highlights the need to consider research efforts that rather seek to understand

Global prevalence of themes

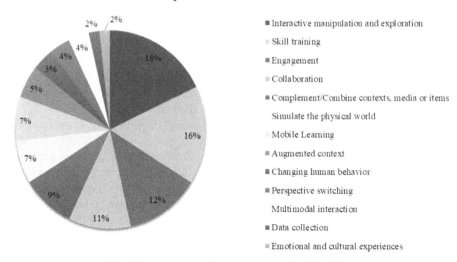

Fig. 5. Prevalence of themes of uses of ImT for SRL.

the possible approaches to support SRL and its different components in immersive environments. Which research methodologies and instruments are suitable to assess/measure SRL in immersive learning is with a question emerging from this work.

Most of the descriptions focus on exploration activities, flexible, free interaction with the environment and resources, self-choices, customizing paths and integration of elements that allow the monitoring of progress, incentive and motivational. This confirms that instructors need to deepen their "know-how" about immersive learning experiences and how to develop different SRL strategies [6, 7, 13, 16, 17].

Table 6. Summary of uses of VR, AR, MR for SRL

ID	Type (VR, AR, or MR)	Description
P1	VR Multi-user virtual environment (MUVE) in Second Life: Language Lab	Virtual English class: Attend a class by a teacher represented by an avatar. Follow the guidelines of tasks and activities. Interaction with other classmates and teacher (avatars). Visit to realistic scenarios. Participation in task of own choice

(continued)

Table 6. (*continued*)

ID	Type (VR, AR, or MR)	Description
P2	VR 3D virtual museum and digital environment	Experimentation of 3D spaces to acquire knowledge and use time freely without restrictions. Observation activities and listening information about objects. Conducting a familiarization test (pre-test of knowledge) before taking the actual test. Training to know how to use the material and resources (memory task: memorize knowledge about each virtual sculpture after listening spoken information)
P3	MR Unity + smart mobile device	Freely rotate their bodies to observe from different angles and interact with the content. Content exposed in dialog format. Motivational test items
P4	MR History-related 360° videos	Explicit SRL training to develop cognitive strategies. They learned the terms and functionalities of cognitive and metacognitive strategies. Guidance and practice these strategies to analyse 360° videos through exercises. Use of a digital poster for introduction and class discussion
P5	MR Tablet camera to see their real-life surrounding	Thoughtful paper mock-ups and still screenshots depicting the weather in different outdoor seasons. Items that show progress by providing feedback and rewards for students exploring the environment (incentives). Recording and analysis of feedback to assess expectations. Access to own progress and that of colleagues. Sharing information that you believe will be of interest to others. Discussion of learning options. Flexibility in exploring and interacting with content: choose what you want to learn
P6	AR The Anat_Hub: AR mode, 3D mode; glossary, and quiz features	Interaction with content on information panels. Presentation of contents in an organized way that facilitates the organization and processing of information. Self-tests. Opportunity to choose the format of the material you want to use for the study

(continued)

Table 6. (*continued*)

ID	Type (VR, AR, or MR)	Description
P7	VR Whiteboard in the VR space; Head-mounted display (HMD); Voice recognition device (VRD)	Personalized experiences, creating an avatar that reflects the user (physical size and movement). Display of content with automatic change (changes after a while). Control over pause time, so the user can see the content again. Acquisition of phonemes through self-feedback. Access to scores (evaluation)
P8	VR Chinese folk art performance multimedia system	Selection and management of material, instructions, and personal information according to their performance needs
P9	VR Virtual world: Crystal Island-Outbreak	Self-discovery through exploration of the virtual world. Interaction with characters who are experts. Space to formulate questions, generate hypotheses, collect data, and test hypotheses. Completion and submission of a diagnosis. Provision of score (feedback) with reward for having efficiently reached the objectives. Awareness of the overall goal. Solving complex problems
P10	MR VR headsets with smartphones	Collaborative activities to promote scientific intrinsic values. Content transmission. Exploration of virtual spaces. Scene observation, synchronization, and activation of instructions for acquiring detailed information. Resource involvement
P11	VR OpenSim: Wireless Island	Interactive simulations. Exploration of learning contents. Experimentation with constructions and can edit objects. Learning materials available at specific locations

5   Limitations

This literature review had one specific focus and consequently only included papers explicitly mentioning the terms "self-regulated learning" and "immersion" in their abstracts. So, papers that worked on SRL or immersion by other terms may have been excluded. Also, the final corpus is small, so results generalization is limited. We recommend that future literature reviews include other search terms related to SRL and VR, AR, MR. In addition, we recommend considering SRL more broadly, by considering not only SRL wholly, but also the individual SRL strategies (e.g., time management, seeking help, monitoring, etc.).

6 Conclusions and Final Thoughts

This work showed that uses of VR, AR, and MR to support the development of SRL has increased in recent years, in various fields and mostly in higher education, but also in other contexts. We identified 18 uses, 5 of which are not found in the reference framework. They were also found to be absent in combination of high narrative immersion with significant levels of system-based and agency-based immersion. Despite this interest and increased use, explicit details of the instructional design and implementation of the found uses to develop SRL strategies are vague, focusing essentially on flexibility, freedom of self-exploration, interaction, manipulation of spaces and resources, feedback elements, and motivational approaches.

The studies lack details on how to support development of SRL strategies (such as planning, managing, seeking help, transformation, review, self-assessment, etc.). This points towards opportunities to explore these uses and describe them to support replication and application studies. There is also a clear need to study the applicability to SRL of uses of immersive environments associated with high narrative immersion that integrates significant levels of the other dimensions the phenomenon of immersion.

Acknowledgment. This work is financially supported by National Funds through FCT – Fundação para a Ciência e a Tecnologia, I.P., under the project UIDB/00194/2020. D. Pedrosa wishes to thank FCT and CIDTFF - Universidade de Aveiro, Portugal, for Stimulus of Scientific Employment – CEECIND/00986/2017 Individual Support 2017.

References

1. 2020 EDUCAUSE Horizon Report: Teaching and Learning Edition. EDUCAUSE (Association), Louisville, CO [USA] (2020)
2. Suh, A., Prophet, J.: The state of immersive technology research: a literature analysis. Comput. Hum. Behav. **86**, 77–90 (2018). https://doi.org/10.1016/j.chb.2018.04.019
3. Bekele, M.K., Pierdicca, R., Frontoni, E., Malinverni, E.S., Gain, J.: A survey of augmented, virtual, and mixed reality for cultural heritage. J. Comput. Cult. Herit. **11**, 7:1–7:36 (2018). https://doi.org/10.1145/3145534
4. Guo, X., Guo, Y., Liu, Y.: The development of extended reality in education: inspiration from the research literature. Sustainability. **13**, 13776 (2021). https://doi.org/10.3390/su132413776
5. Tang, Y.M., Chau, K.Y., Kwok, A.P.K., Zhu, T., Ma, X.: A systematic review of immersive technology applications for medical practice and education - trends, application areas, recipients, teaching contents, evaluation methods, and performance. Educ. Res. Rev. **35**, 100429 (2022). https://doi.org/10.1016/j.edurev.2021.100429
6. Makransky, G., Mayer, R.E.: Benefits of taking a virtual field trip in immersive virtual reality: evidence for the immersion principle in multimedia learning. Educ. Psychol. Rev. **34**, 1771–1798 (2022). https://doi.org/10.1007/s10648-022-09675-4
7. Pellas, N., Mystakidis, S., Kazanidis, I.: Immersive virtual reality in K-12 and higher education: a systematic review of the last decade scientific literature. Virtual Real. **25**, 835–861 (2021). https://doi.org/10.1007/s10055-020-00489-9
8. Garzón, J., Pavón, J., Baldiris, S.: Systematic review and meta-analysis of augmented reality in educational settings. Virtual Real. **23**, 447–459 (2019). https://doi.org/10.1007/s10055-019-00379-9

9. Akçayır, M., Akçayır, G.: Advantages and challenges associated with augmented reality for education: a systematic review of the literature. Educ. Res. Rev. **20**, 1–11 (2017). https://doi.org/10.1016/j.edurev.2016.11.002

10. Crompton, H., Bernacki, M., Greene, J.A.: Psychological foundations of emerging technologies for teaching and learning in higher education. Curr. Opin. Psychol. **36**, 101–105 (2020). https://doi.org/10.1016/j.copsyc.2020.04.011

11. Makransky, G., Petersen, G.B.: The cognitive affective model of immersive learning (CAMIL): a theoretical research-based model of learning in immersive virtual reality. Educ. Psychol. Rev. **33**, 937–958 (2021). https://doi.org/10.1007/s10648-020-09586-2

12. Kaplan, A.D., Cruit, J., Endsley, M., Beers, S.M., Sawyer, B.D., Hancock, P.A.: The effects of virtual reality, augmented reality, and mixed reality as training enhancement methods: a meta-analysis. Hum. Factors **63**, 706–726 (2021). https://doi.org/10.1177/0018720820904229

13. Dunleavy, M., Dede, C., Mitchell, R.: Affordances and limitations of immersive participatory augmented reality simulations for teaching and learning. J. Sci. Educ. Technol. **18**, 7–22 (2009). https://doi.org/10.1007/s10956-008-9119-1

14. Makransky, G., Wismer, P., Mayer, R.E.: A gender matching effect in learning with pedagogical agents in an immersive virtual reality science simulation. J. Comput. Assist. Learn. **35**, 349–358 (2019). https://doi.org/10.1111/jcal.12335

15. Makransky, G., Terkildsen, T.S., Mayer, R.E.: Adding immersive virtual reality to a science lab simulation causes more presence but less learning. Learn. Instr. **60**, 225–236 (2019). https://doi.org/10.1016/j.learninstruc.2017.12.007

16. Pirker, J., Dengel, A., Holly, M., Safikhani, S.: Virtual reality in computer science education: a systematic review. In: Proceedings of the 26th ACM Symposium on Virtual Reality Software and Technology, pp. 1–8. Association for Computing Machinery, New York (2020)

17. Wagner, C., Liu, L.: Creating Immersive Learning Experiences: A Pedagogical Design Perspective. In: Hui, A., Wagner, C. (eds.) Creative and Collaborative Learning through Immersion, pp. 71–87. Springer, Cham (2021). https://doi.org/10.1007/978-3-030-72216-6_5

18. Pintrich, P.R.: A conceptual framework for assessing motivation and self-regulated learning in college students. Educ. Psychol. Rev. **16**, 385–407 (2004). https://doi.org/10.1007/s10648-004-0006-x

19. Zimmerman, B.J.: From cognitive modeling to self-regulation: a social cognitive career path. Educ. Psychol. **48**, 135–147 (2013). https://doi.org/10.1080/00461520.2013.794676

20. Panadero, E.: A review of self-regulated learning: six models and four directions for research. Front. Psychol. **8**, 422 (2017). https://doi.org/10.3389/fpsyg.2017.00422

21. Pedrosa, D., Cravino, J.P., Morgado, L. (eds.): e-SimProgramming: planificar, conceber e acompanhar atividades didáticas online de engenharia de software. Universidade Aberta, Lisboa, Portugal (2022)

22. Broadbent, J., Poon, W.L.: Self-regulated learning strategies & academic achievement in online higher education learning environments: a systematic review. Internet High. Educ. **27**, 1–13 (2015). https://doi.org/10.1016/j.iheduc.2015.04.007

23. Kramarski, B., Heaysman, O.: A conceptual framework and a professional development model for supporting teachers' "triple SRL–SRT processes" and promoting students' academic outcomes. Educ. Psychol. **56**, 298–311 (2021). https://doi.org/10.1080/00461520.2021.1985502

24. Dengel, A.: What is immersive learning? In: 2022 8th International Conference of the Immersive Learning Research Network (iLRN), pp. 1–5 (2022)

25. Nilsson, N.C., Nordahl, R., Serafin, S.: Immersion revisited: a review of existing definitions of immersion and their relation to different theories of presence. Hum. Technol. **12**, 108–134 (2016). https://doi.org/10.17011/ht/urn.201611174652

26. Agrawal, S., Simon, A., Bech, S., Bærentsen, K., Forchhammer, S.: Defining immersion: literature review and implications for research on audiovisual experiences. J. Audio Eng. Soc. **68**, 404–417 (2020). https://doi.org/10.17743/jaes.2020.0039

27. Beck, D., Morgado, L., O'Shea, P.: Finding the gaps about uses of immersive learning environments: a survey of surveys. J. Univers. Comput. Sci. **26**(8), 1043–1073 (2020)

28. Maas, M.J., Hughes, J.M.: Virtual, augmented and mixed reality in K–12 education: a review of the literature. Technol. Pedagogy Educ. **29**, 231–249 (2020). https://doi.org/10.1080/147 5939X.2020.1737210

29. Milgram, P., Kishino, F.: A Taxonomy of Mixed Reality Visual Displays. https://search.ieice. org/bin/summary.php?id=e77-d_12_1321

30. Carmigniani, J., Furht, B., Anisetti, M., Ceravolo, P., Damiani, E., Ivkovic, M.: Augmented reality technologies, systems and applications. Multimed. Tools Appl. **51**, 341–377 (2011). https://doi.org/10.1007/s11042-010-0660-6

31. Flavián, C., Ibáñez-Sánchez, S., Orús, C.: The impact of virtual, augmented and mixed reality technologies on the customer experience. J. Bus. Res. **100**, 547–560 (2019). https://doi.org/ 10.1016/j.jbusres.2018.10.050

32. Rauschnabel, P.A., Felix, R., Hinsch, C., Shahab, H., Alt, F.: What is XR? towards a framework for augmented and virtual reality. Comput. Hum. Behav. **133**, 107289 (2022). https://doi.org/ 10.1016/j.chb.2022.107289

33. Skarbez, R., Smith, M., Whitton, M.C.: Revisiting milgram and Kishino's reality-virtuality continuum. Front. Virtual Real. **2** (2021)

34. Pan, Z., Cheok, A.D., Yang, H., Zhu, J., Shi, J.: Virtual reality and mixed reality for virtual learning environments. Comput. Graph. **30**, 20–28 (2006). https://doi.org/10.1016/j.cag.2005. 10.004

35. Hughes, C.E., Stapleton, C.B., Hughes, D.E., Smith, E.M.: Mixed reality in education, entertainment, and training. IEEE Comput. Graph. Appl. **25**, 24–30 (2005). https://doi.org/10. 1109/MCG.2005.139

36. Kitchenham, B.A., Budgen, D., Brereton, P.: Evidence-Based Software Engineering and Systematic Reviews. Chapman & Hall/CRC (2015)

37. Braun, V., Clarke, V.: Using thematic analysis in psychology. Qual. Res. Psychol. **3**, 77–101 (2006). https://doi.org/10.1191/1478088706qp063oa

38. Pedrosa, D., Morgado, L., Beck, D.: Companion dataset for paper "Immersive Learning Environments for Self-Regulation of Learning: A Literature Review" (2023). https://zenodo. org/record/7568158

Technology for Content Creation

Co-creation and Personalization
of an Immersive Web Environment

Bárbara Cleto⬤, Carlos Santos⁽⊠⁾⬤, and Mário Vairinhos⬤

DigiMedia Research Center, University of Aveiro, Aveiro, Portugal
{barbara.cleto,carlossantos,mariov}@ua.pt

Abstract. This article presents the design of a study that aims to explore whether the fact that students, in collaboration with their teachers (or teacher), co-create Immersive Web Environments (IWE), enables them to reflect on and analyse the way they learn. Therefore, it is intended to understand whether the co-creation and personalization of an IWE can promote metacognition. The article focuses mainly on the planning and design of the experience to be implemented. As well as the definition (elaboration or adaptation) of the data collection instruments, based on the literature review carried out so far and the perceptions of a group of teachers, regarding the construction and customization of immersive web environments, resulting from the training workshop. In the training workshop, teachers had the opportunity to learn about and explore immersive web environments so that they can integrate them into the teaching and learning process. They conceptualized and designed didactic - pedagogical activities for the environment, having customized the IWE according to the planned pedagogical activity, to teach the different contents related to their subject, as well as their subject areas.

Keywords: Immersive Web Environments · personalization · co-creation · metacognition

1 Introduction

Classroom dynamics are changing, teachers are looking for alternatives to the expositive classes [1]. Learning by doing has become the option in a process of co-production of knowledge and new approaches have emerged [1], the active methodologies. The student while participating becomes an active creator of knowledge and not just a passive receiver of information. While creating, they learn. They builds mental models [2] that allow them to think before their actions and reflect on their own actions, based on the interactions and feedback obtained [3].

Immersive Web Environments (IWE), powered by WebXR technology, facilitate access to online content, which can be accessed by a web browser or experienced on devices with Virtual Reality and Augmented Reality content capabilities [4, 5], allowing real-time interaction with virtual objects and other users. These environments can promote and develop (in students) the "four Cs of learning": Creativity and Innovation; Critical Thinking and Problem Solving; Communication; Collaboration [6] as they

© ICST Institute for Computer Sciences, Social Informatics and Telecommunications Engineering 2024
Published by Springer Nature Switzerland AG 2024. All Rights Reserved
D. Crawford et al. (Eds.): TIE 2023, LNICST 575, pp. 85–93, 2024.
https://doi.org/10.1007/978-3-031-59383-3_6

enable students to learn in a place where the risk of complex tasks is minimized [7, 8], through simulation capabilities [7], motivating them to reflect carefully and creatively on their learning [9].

The fact that there is a greater sense of (shared) presence and greater social interaction can enhance collaboration, making the work more dynamic and engaging [10]. These environments enable and promote the creation of learning communities, where the design process is possible with the collaboration between students from various institutions. If they are connected and have similar access, they can interact among peers, or even extend the collaborations between academia, industry and community [8]. It allows students to be at home and learn in an environment similar to their traditional classrooms, without losing the ability to learn at their own pace, thus eliminating problems of time, distance and availability. In addition to enabling immersive and experiential, just-in-time learning, which uses concrete but exploratory experiences that engage the various senses [8].

2 Related Work

The analysis of some projects allowed us to bring to this stage of the research the most relevant elements of each of them. It should be noted that only those that are of most interest to the project phase in which the team is currently, research design and implementation, will be indicated.

One of the many studies [11] consulted, aimed to explore whether the fact of students creating 3D worlds in virtual reality increased their autonomy for learning, in this case of a foreign language (English). The conceptualization of this and other studies [6] reporting on a pilot in which secondary school students create 360° VR learning resources for primary school students, allowed not only to structure and redefine some aspects of the research design, but also to "validate" some of the instruments that were initially thought to be used and to redefine new ones. The conceptual basis of the study [6], also allowed us to reflect on some dimensions that can be explored that are related to the 4 C's of 21st Century Skills, namely content mastery (how they acquire knowledge and transfer it to real world situations), critical thinking and problem solving, as well as motivation to persist, collaboration and peer-to-peer work (conflict and project management) and how they use teacher feedback to monitor and guide their own learning (one of the aspects related to metacognition).

One of the studies consulted [12], describes an experiment carried out in 2020, where two spaces were developed specifically for the intervention, and two physical spaces were modelled, a park and a replica of a real classroom, where users could interact with the placed multimedia elements, namely increase their size, to facilitate their visualization. Three studies were carried out: a workshop for educators, a session in an informal learning context and another in a formal context. The authors describe the data obtained, the problems encountered and how they solved them during the various sessions. There is a "Lessons learnt" section, very useful for this research and which will be considered during its preparation, regarding the design of the space, they should have few 3D objects; simplify the sharing of content; switch off audio at the beginning; share URLs in the chat and use invitation-only links. Regarding the planning and preparation of the sessions, it should be considered that time is needed to get used to IWE, so a room should be created with detailed instructions for participants to learn the controls, the way to navigate, and presentation features on IWE.

3   Project Research

The theme addressed in this article was initially tested in an attempt to "escape" from the 2D platforms (Zoom, Teams, Classroom), (students wanted to escape from 2D platforms), used during the pandemic [13–15]. After this experience, the students started to design their own classrooms, and the idea emerged to study the impact and appropriation that the students make of the immersive web environments, because they were participating in activities that resulted in a process of co-authorship of the design of the space.

The current research project consists in creating and developing an educational experience that allows students and teachers to co-create immersive virtual environments to explore how they can use these environments and create their own contexts for learning one or several themes (for example, mathematics and physics teachers and their students can create an environment to explore the laws of motion and solve the associated equations), participating in the codesign of the development of the "classroom" space. It is also intended to verify the impact of the experiment on students' metacognition.

The research design underwent several changes as the literature review became more theme-oriented and after the analysis of the state of the art regarding already existing works and projects, thus establishing the scientific basis to support and outline the experience to be implemented. It also underwent changes based on the results obtained in the training workshop.

3.1   Initial Proposal of the Research Project

For this project, the following research question was formulated: "What is the impact on the educational experience of the involvement and incorporation of primary and secondary school students in processes of co-creation of virtual environments?". In this way, the aim is to understand, based on the experience, which will take place in a classroom context, and the perspective of teachers and students, the use of IWE, the customization of these environments and how students appropriate them, by having participated in their creation, i.e., is intended to understand the impact and challenges of the combination of these three vectors: IWE, customization, co-creation.

Research Design
The initial phase of the project took place from April to July 2021, and considering: i) the initial research question (which has been modified), ii) the intended objectives, and iii) in articulation with the fieldwork (initially planned), it configured a case study, following a quantitative and qualitative approach, more exploratory and descriptive, where elementary and secondary school teachers and students create and customise an IWE. The evaluation of the experience to be planned would have to analyse and compare the impact on the educational experience between students who, participated in the co-creation of the environment and used the environments they created (group A) and those

who only used the environment, created by classmates and/or teachers (group B). The comparative analysis of the two groups would allow the discovery of new impacts and challenges arising from the use of IWE, in the teaching/learning process, in a bottom-up logic, i.e., after analyzing the data, one can start building a theory [16] and it should take place in a real context (classroom).

Thus, the research is a case study in which both quantitative and qualitative methodologies are used [17], given its characteristics which focus on a specific and unique situation, not aiming at generalization. Considering the particularities of the study, its nature will be mixed, combining qualitative and quantitative data [18, 19], enabling the existence of a complementarity of data collection methods, which allows for a better perception and understanding of the object under study [20]. Multiple data should be collected, and different strategies, approaches and methods used in complementarity of strengths and weaknesses [21].

Data Collection Instruments
The following data collection tools were used: teachers' notes [20], interview surveys to teachers, questionnaire surveys to students and the creation of a focus group. The focus group was intended to clarify some aspects that raised doubts, since the focus group combines interview and observation [22], allowing the researcher to collect the participants' opinions [23].

Indirect observation (audiovisual recording), which allows for a diversified collection and use of qualitative and quantitative data, enabling data triangulation, thus enhancing the validity and reliability of interpretations and conclusions [17, 24, 25]. Other records, such as reflections made by teachers and students, the environments created within the experience and training and other material that is produced (records and/or descriptions arising from observation), can also be used.

It is necessary to consider all the procedures related to the compliance with legal and ethical issues for data collection, namely: informed consent of all the intervening parties, authorizations to carry out the study and the guarantee of anonymity [18] and confidentiality of the data collected.

Participants
In this initial stage of the research, the participants were not defined, their selection was made during a Training Workshop, where primary and secondary school teachers, from all subject areas, were challenged to participate in the research. This group of teachers should choose the students who will create the environments (convenience sampling). One of the groups (A) will design the environments, while another group (B), will only use the environments created by group A.

It was already expected that the fact that the selection of the participants was made in the workshop, would have some inconveniences, namely: the size of the participant's group, conditioned by the voluntary participation of the teachers and also by the constraints imposed by the schools, since the intention is that the teachers are the ones who choose the students who will participate, as well as the activities they will develop with their students. The need for more time (in addition to the hours planned for the training) for students to create and design the spaces where they will develop their own activities. Or it may be necessary, since the appropriation and use of the space by the two groups will be compared, to have sessions where group A explains and guides group B in the space they have personalized.

The training workshop, accredited by the Scientific-Pedagogical Council for Continuing Education and facilitated by the group of researchers, took place in 2022, and served to capacitate teachers, introducing them to the IWE and enabling them to develop pedagogical activities in these IWE.

Procedures
In this phase, the research focused on the planning of the training sessions, the production of support materials to be made available to the trainees and essentially the definition of data collection instruments to be tested. The training workshop allowed to readjust the data collection instruments that had initially been planned.

Training Workshop (Edition One)
The training workshop took place between March and June 2022. As previously mentioned, the training workshop allowed to identify and choose the teachers who will implement the study, based on the performance of the proposed activities during the various training sessions, but also to enable teachers to get to know, get used to, understand the potential of these IWE and reflect on the contributions that these environments can bring to improve the teaching and learning process. It also served to test the data collection instruments. The training included a part in which teachers were instructed how to customize and build their own environments, according to the planned pedagogical activities. However, rather than focusing on technology, the focus was on pedagogy and how to explore and integrate IWE in the educational context.

After analyzing the work done by the teachers, it was found that most of them chose to use the templates offered by the platforms used, only customizing the spaces, for the pedagogical activities they planned and then implemented with the students. It was also found that the majority did not co-create these spaces with the students.

The teachers were then asked about their options, the questions were divided into two groups: i) What was the teacher's role in the design of the pedagogical experience and ii) questions related to the platform and customization tools.

Regarding the role of the teacher in the design of the pedagogical experience, we tried to understand: i) Was the teacher the only facilitator, thus influencing the creative/constructive process of the space? ii) Was there student intervention, and did the teacher influence the students' creative/constructive process, or did the teacher just "follow" student instructions? iii) The teacher had no influence on the process and the IWE was entirely constructed by the students.

Most of them mentioned that, given the fact that it was their first experience with this kind of environment, they were responsible for its creation and development, using already existing resources, thus it was possible for them to explore and experiment the potentialities of immersive environments. After that, the students had access to the environment, having been sent the link of the room, to explore and extend a theme worked with them in classroom context. However, it was found that some teachers made the activities available for the students to do, while other teachers listened and discussed the proposals for action, asking the students for proposals of the work they (students) had done, to be included in the immersive room created by the teachers.

They mention that they would have preferred the students to build the space themselves, but, since the students had never worked with these immersive environments and there was not much time to explore them with the students, they also indicate that the school's computer equipment is obsolete and does not meet the minimum requirements for these platforms to work satisfactorily.

Regarding the questions related to platforms and customization tools, an attempt was made to understand, if the fact that there are templates and several 3D objects, limits the creativity and conditions the choices or if the students and/or teachers used objects created by them in other 3D modelling platforms.

Teachers consider that not providing any template would make the use of the platform much more constraining or even impossible. They mention that this would certainly depend on the objective that is intended to be achieved. If the goal is to create a specific environment, there may be some restrictions, but if the goal is to create a room with other types of content (e.g. presentations, videos created by students, ….), it does not seem to be a limitation. It is possible to customize them to give a more personal touch, within the templates provided, it allows you to make choices. There is always the possibility to personalize them a bit, thus giving them a more personal touch.

3.2 Changes to the Research Project

With the knowledge of the participants and with the explanation of what is intended to be done, it was possible to define the working groups that will continue with the researchers, from October 2022, in the implementation phase of the project.

Many teachers wanted to create their own spaces. In fact, this was one of the first questions that came up during the training. In September 2022, teachers were contacted again to find out if they were still interested in collaborating with researchers in the co-creation of IWEs. However, and considering that only one teacher showed availability to continue collaborating with the research, it was then launched a new edition of the training workshop, to see if in this new group, there are more teachers interested in participating in the study. It was realized that it was necessary to reformulate the proposal presented, both in terms of methodology and in terms of simplification of data collection instruments and research question that became "What is the impact of incorporating in co-creation processes students' involvement in the educational experience of primary and secondary education and immersive web environments?".

Tools

Teachers will be asked to record the process of creating the worlds and to make a written record (multimodal narratives) of what is happening. Students will be asked to use the using thinking-out-loud (TOL) protocols [26] to understand how students construct and why they construct. Thus, the instruments to be used, besides the ones previously mentioned, are also considered IWE (again the use of the platform will not be conditioned). The platforms used allow us to personalize the avatar, except for Spatial [27] which allows us to use our own image. They allow communication by chat. The only one that has its own tool for construction is Mozilla Hubs [28], which has Spoke [29], but all of them allow the construction in other tools (Blender [30], Tinkercad [31], among others) and their integration. In the training, IWE Frame VR [32] was essentially approached. All platforms have predefined scenarios, to which 3D models, images, videos, and other multimedia elements can be added.

Training Workshop (Edition Two)

The training workshop took place between March and June 2023. Until the new edition of the workshop, the research focused on the continuation of the literature review and the analysis of the results of the previous workshop, which enabled the reformulation of some contents and materials in the reformulation of the research planning. In the second edition there was a greater concern in empowering teachers to integrate these environments in the teaching and learning process. For this purpose, the sessions were reformulated so that they had more time to design pedagogical activities to use within the environments and consequently build/customize the immersive web environments to teach the contents according to the subject area.

Although the workshop has not finished yet, it is possible to verify that teachers follow the same pattern of workshop one and tend to use the templates that the platforms provide. The same questionnaire of workshop one was applied (i) What is the role of the Teacher in the design of the pedagogical experience and ii) questions related to the platform and customization tools. The answers obtained show that teachers want to know, explore, test and therefore they are the ones who create the space, providing the link to students to help personalize the room. The teachers mention that they assigned the role of administrators to the students, giving them total freedom to build their spaces, only indicating which "slots" each group should have. They mention that no two spaces are the same and some students have placed images, videos, gifts, objects, presentations, made by them. However, they indicate difficulties in inserting and loading resources, especially when several students try to access and use them simultaneously. They indicate that students found the space welcoming, and even said that classes should be taught in those spaces.

A group of students started building their own IWE spaces from scratch. Regarding the issues related to platforms and customization tools, they considered that the fact that templates already existed did not limit creativity. Since the purpose of using these tools in a school context should be as easy as possible, considering that the subject programs are large, and the time spent building environments from "zero" is a constraint. The different existing templates allowed them to achieve the objectives they had set themselves. They also mention that they did not use objects "outside" the platform, but the students did, besides adding objects, some of them built them.

4   Final Remarks

This article describes the development process of the study that is intended to be implemented, exploring how this process of co-creation of IWE between students and teachers. The steps for the development of the current research project were described and the decisions taken were grounded, as well as the theoretical framework that supports the research. Some of the procedures that can be adopted were addressed, as well as the data collection tools to be used for later analysis and evaluation of the experience.

The aim is to study the educational potential of immersive virtual environments, Immersive Web [4] designing activities and customizing these environments, according to the various themes, in a process of collaborative co-creation, among students, of primary and secondary education, to assess the appropriation that students make of the space created by them and/or created by their colleagues and/or teachers. There was a concern to collect some data to assess how teachers use them in their teaching practice. The data shows that teachers need more training to feel comfortable in their use, however they consider that there is a huge potential in their use.

Acknowledgments. To the teachers who agreed to collaborate and provided the data requested by the researchers, contributing to the study of the use of IWE in an educational context.

References

1. Cleto, B.: Learning Systems and Gamification: Blending Augmented and Virtual Reality With Gamification Strategies, pp. 54–67 (2021). https://services.igi-global.com/res olvedoi/resolve.aspx?doi=10.4018/978-1-7998-7472-0.ch004. https://doi.org/10.4018/978-1-7998-7472-0.ch004

2. Trust, T., Maloy, R.W., Edwards, S.: Learning through making: emerging and expanding designs for college classes. TechTrends **62**(1), 19–28 (2018). https://doi.org/10.1007/S11 528-017-0214-0/FIGURES/3

3. Veenman, M.V.J., Van Hout-Wolters, B.H.A.M., Afflerbach, P.: Metacognition and learning: conceptual and methodological considerations. Metacognition Learn. **1**(1), 3–14 (2006). https://doi.org/10.1007/S11409-006-6893-0

4. MacIntyre, B., Smith, T.F.: Thoughts on the future of WebXR and the immersive web. In: Adjunct Proceedings - 2018 IEEE International Symposium on Mixed and Augmented Reality, ISMAR-Adjunct 2018, pp. 338–342 (2018). https://doi.org/10.1109/ISMAR-ADJUNCT. 2018.00099

5. Rodríguez, F.C., Dal Peraro, M., Abriata, L.A.: Democratizing interactive, immersive experiences for science education with WebXR. Nat. Comput. Sci. **1**(10), 631–632 (2021). https://doi.org/10.1038/s43588-021-00142-8

6. Southgate, E., Grant, S., Ostrowski, S., Norwood, A., Williams, M., Tafazoli, D.: School students creating a virtual reality learning resource for children. In: Proceedings - 2022 IEEE Conference on Virtual Reality and 3D User Interfaces Abstracts and Workshops, VRW 2022, pp. 261–266 (2022). https://doi.org/10.1109/VRW55335.2022.00060

7. Correia, A., Fonseca, B., Paredes, H., Martins, P., Morgado, L.: Computer-simulated 3D virtual environments in collaborative learning and training: meta-review, refinement, and roadmap. In: Sivan, Y. (ed.) Handbook on 3D3C Platforms, pp. 403–440. Springer, Cham (2016). https://doi.org/10.1007/978-3-319-22041-3_15

8. Ziker, C., Truman, B., Dodds, H.: Cross reality (XR): challenges and opportunities across the spectrum. In: Innovative Learning Environments in STEM Higher Education, pp. 55–77. Nature Publishing Group (2021). https://doi.org/10.1007/978-3-030-58948-6_4

9. Papanastasiou, G., Drigas, A., Skianis, C., Lytras, M., Papanastasiou, E.: Virtual and augmented reality effects on K-12, higher and tertiary education students' twenty-first century skills. Virtual Real. **23**(4), 425–436 (2019). https://doi.org/10.1007/S10055-018-0363-2/TAB LES/2

10. Reeves: Design of learning spaces in 3D virtual worlds: an empirical investigation of Second Life, pp. 29–55 (2013). https://doi.org/10.4324/9780203723135-8

11. Yeh, Y.L., Lan, Y.J.: Fostering student autonomy in English learning through creations in a 3D virtual world. Education Tech. Research Dev. **66**(3), 693–708 (2018). https://doi.org/10.1007/S11423-017-9566-6/FIGURES/5

12. Williams, S., Enatsky, R., Gillcash, H., Murphy, J.J., Gracanin, D.: Immersive technology in the public school classroom: when a class meets. In: Proceedings of 2021 7th International Conference of the Immersive Learning Research Network, iLRN 2021 (2021). https://doi.org/10.23919/iLRN52045.2021.9459371

13. Cleto, B., Carvalho, R., Ferreira, M.: Work in progress: immersive web environments to support pedagogical activities in formal contexts. In: Auer, M.E., Tsiatsos, T. (eds.) IMCL 2021. LNNS, vol. 411, pp. 703–710. Springer, Cham (2022). https://doi.org/10.1007/978-3-030-96296-8_63

14. Cleto, B., Ferreira, M., Carvalho, R.: An analysis of interactions of secondary school students in virtual environments. In: ACM International Conference Proceeding Series (2021). https://doi.org/10.1145/3483529.3483678

15. Cleto, B., Carvalho, R., Ferreira, M.: Students' perceptions exploring a WebXR learning environment. In: Brooks, E., Sjöberg, J., Møller, A.K. (eds.) DLI 2021. Lecture Notes of the Institute for Computer Sciences, Social-Informatics and Telecommunications Engineering, LNICST, vol. 435, pp. 230–241. Springer, Cham (2022). https://doi.org/10.1007/978-3-031-06675-7_17

16. Lincoln, Y.S.: Emerging criteria for quality in qualitative and interpretive research. Qual. Inq. 1(3), 275–289 (1995). https://doi.org/10.1177/107780049500100301

17. Yin, R.: Estudo de caso: planejamento e método, 3a ed. Porto Alegre (2005)

18. Creswell, J.: Qualitative Inquiry and Research Design (2017 edition) | Open Library (2007). https://openlibrary.org/books/OL28633749M/Qualitative_Inquiry_and_Research_Design. Accessed 06 June 2021

19. Creswell, J., et al.: RESEARCH (2006)

20. Bogdan, R.C., Knopp Biklen, S., Boston, B.: Third Edition Qualitative Research for Education An Introduction to Theory and Methods (1998). www.abacon.com. Accessed 07 June 2021

21. Onwuegbuzie, A.J., Johnson, R.B.: The validity issue in mixed research. Res. Sch. 13(1), 48–63 (2006)

22. Teddlie, C., Tashakkori, A.: Foundations of mixed methods research: integrating quantitative and qualitative approaches in the Social and Behavioral Sciences. Thousand Oaks (2009)

23. Krueger, R.A., Casey, M.A.: Focus Groups: A Practical Guide for Applied Research, 5a. International Educational and Professional Publisher (2015)

24. Flick, U.: Introducción a la investigación cualitativa (2004)

25. Stake, R.E.: Investigación con estudio de casos (1999)

26. Olson, G.M., Duffy, S.A., Mack, R.L.: Thinking-out-loud as a method for studying real-time comprehension processes. In: New Methods in Reading Comprehension Research, pp. 253–286 (2018). https://doi.org/10.4324/9780429505379-11

27. Spatial - Virtual Spaces That Bring Us Together. https://spatial.io/. Accessed 22 Nov 2021

28. Hubs - Private, virtual 3D worlds in your browser. https://hubs.mozilla.com/. Accessed 22 Nov 2021

29. Spoke by Mozilla. https://hubs.mozilla.com/spoke/. Accessed 22 Nov 2021

30. blender.org - Home of the Blender project - Free and Open 3D Creation Software. https://www.blender.org/. Accessed 22 Nov 2021

31. Tinkercad | Create 3D digital designs with online CAD | Tinkercad. https://www.tinkercad.com/. Accessed 22 Nov 2021

32. Frame - Immersive Meetings, Classes, Events. https://learn.framevr.io/. Accessed 22 Nov 2021

The Meta-Stage: Utilizing Metaverse-Enabling Technologies for Hybrid Co-presence Experiences

Rameshnath Krishnasamy[1]([⊠]) [iD], Peter Vistisen[1] [iD], Lana Tankosa Nikolic[2],
Lars Hemmingsen[2], and Martina Scarpelli[2]

[1] Aalborg University, Rendsburggade 14, 9000 Aalborg, Denmark
krishnasamy@id.aau.dk
[2] White Hole Theater, Ammunitionsvej 4, 8800 Viborg, Denmark

Abstract. This paper introduces the concept for 'The Meta-stage' – a concept for live performance arts through the so-called 'Metaverse'. The Metaverse can be seen as the effort to further facilitate the digital transformation in a scale potentially comparable to the WWW protocol - a vision of an immersive Internet as a unified, persistent, and shared space, with the Meta-stage being a subsequent specialized part of this whole. The paper introduces how the iterations of the Meta-stage have evolved, and how the engagement with the cultural sector, including performing and visual arts such as theater and live performances with an audience, is becoming entangled in the Metaverse. Through a research-through-design overview, the paper explores, which design principles can be established for cultural and public events in the Metaverse?

Keywords: Hybrid Co-Experience · Extended Reality (XR) · Metaverse

1 Introduction

The term 'Metaverse' finds its origin in Neal Stephenson's 1992 science fiction novel, 'Snow Crash,' where it denotes a virtual reality space in which users engage within a computer-generated environment (Stephenson, 1992). Despite the widespread use of this term, a universally accepted definition of a metaverse remains elusive, with interpretations varying from a lifelogging space to a mirror world (Almoqbel et al., 2022; Benedikt, 2008; Narin, 2021).

While some conceptualize the metaverse as an ideal vision yet to be fully actualized(Metaverse Standards Forum, 2022; Radoff, 2021; Zyda, 2022), others interrogate how this vision aligns with the virtual worlds that have been the focus of academic study for decades (Almoqbel et al., 2022). The Metaverse is often juxtaposed with a future vision of the internet that transcends the static pages of the World Wide Web, evolving into a dynamic and increasingly immersive environment facilitated by technologies that merge physical and virtual spaces. This transformative initiative endeavors

D. Crawford et al. (Eds.): TIE 2023, LNICST 575, pp. 94–106, 2024.
https://doi.org/10.1007/978-3-031-59383-3_7

to construct a metaverse where individuals can engage in real-time interactions with both each other and computer-generated environments. Thus, the 'metaverse' signifies an extensive, immersive virtual environment, though its exact definition remains fluid and warrants further investigation.

In their paper, 'Defining the Metaverse: A Systematic Literature Review' (Ritterbusch & Teichmann, 2023) Georg David Ritterbusch and Malte Rolf Teichmann describe the metaverse as a three-dimensional online environment wherein users interact within virtual spaces independent of the real world. This description aligns with various academic definitions, both past and current, (Almoqbel et al., 2022; L.-H. Lee et al., 2021; Mystakidis, 2022; Ritterbusch & Teichmann, 2023). Through a comprehensive literature review, they propose the following definition:

Metaverse, a crossword of "meta" (meaning transcendency) and "universe", describes a (decentralized) three-dimensional online environment that is persistent and immersive, in which users represented by avatars can participate socially and economically with each other in a creative and collaborative manner in virtual spaces decoupled from the real physical world (Ritterbusch & Teichmann, 2023, p. 12373).

We use this concise definition as a starting point for understanding the state of the technical and technological arenas in which the current conception of the term Metaverse is situated. Although the concept of *a* Metaverse can be captured in the definition above, the full potential remains uncertain and undetermined, yet to be examined and explored. In other words, a *true* Metaverse does not yet exist, as none of the existing virtual worlds are sufficiently decentralized or support a creator economy to a significant degree, which is repeated as core parts of realizing a Metaverse (Almoqbel et al., 2022; Metaverse Standards Forum, 2022; Ritterbusch & Teichmann, 2023). Although the infrastructure is not yet fully developed, it is clear that the Metaverse and the broad field of standalone and interconnected technologies are already present in many different contexts (Ritterbusch & Teichmann, 2023). Emerging technologies such as Extended Reality, 5G connectivity, and Artificial Intelligence have moved the frontier of the Metaverse closer at an increasing speed (S.-M. Park & Kim, 2022; Wang et al., 2022). This technological development is parallel to the increasing level of interest and investment from big tech corporations (Kraus et al., 2022; Rospigliosi, 2022). This engagement entails, that while the fully operationalized vision of the metaverse has yet to be developed, and corporations still have no definitive proposal for how to adopt and collaborate across (still) proprietary platforms, the next frontier of the internet is on the horizon.

Given the recent surge in interest and media attention, it is sensible to explore individual potentials to inform a unified Metaverse infrastructure. This paper directs its focus towards the cultural sector, with the aim of examining past, present and the inevitable future potentials for this sector. The cultural sector, which includes many performing and visual arts such as theatre and similar live performances with an audience, will also be entangled in the Metaverse through enabling technologies (Dixon, 2006; Jernigan et al., 2009). Creators have long combined digital technologies with live performances (Dixon, 2006; Jernigan et al., 2009; Sargeant, 2013), and more recent examples show how audience participation and performative interactions can be part of a live theatre performance that encourages social transactions and active participation from the audience. Theatre is but one example within the cultural sector where Metaverse technologies will enter as a future part of the performance, and one which there is prior knowledge to build upon (Dixon, 2006; Jernigan et al., 2009; Mystakidis, 2022; Simpson & Foster, 2022). It is reasonable to assume that other areas, such as participatory decision processes, virtual town meetings, citizen panels and World Cafés will also adopt Metaverse technologies, over time. Within this space the next section will introduce the study's approach to addressing the cultural sector through a specific Metaverse-enabling platform concept.

1.1 Introducing the Meta-Stage: Investigating Isolated Instantiations of the Metaverse Infrastructure

Our aim is to investigate how emerging Metaverse-enabling technologies might benefit the cultural sector. Our approach is a research-through-design study centered around the conceptual framing of several technologies collectively referred to as 'The Meta-stage'. Through our investigation into a specific aspect of the Metaverse, we aim to provide a foundation for future inquiries into potential design principles for cultural and public events within this digital realm. This exploration carries significant importance, as the guidelines derived from this study could shape the representation, experience, and interaction of cultural events within this rapidly evolving digital landscape.

The cultural sector, encompassing performance and visual arts such as theater and live audience performances, is anticipated to undergo strategic integration with the Metaverse soon. This integration appears plausible considering the escalating digitization of these domains and the immersive capabilities of the Metaverse. With its capacity to facilitate shared, immersive experiences, the Metaverse presents a novel platform for cultural experiences.

This study expands upon the current implementation of the 'Meta-stage'; a combination of Metaverse enabling technologies, carefully selected for live theater performances. So far, the implementation of the Meta-stage has been developed and used for two live performances with a third iteration coming up.

We examine ways in which engagement and immersion can be leveraged to deliver an experience that connects audiences temporally with actors performing in live events, despite spatial separation, by extending on past research into the same context, but with dated technologies, for example (Y.-C. N. Lee et al., 2013; J. Y. Park & Lim, 2022; Reaney, 1999). This context and technological configuration provide potential for transferability and interoperability, elements which a future vision of an interconnected Metaverse could capitalize on. Through a research-through-design overview, the paper explores, which design principles can be established for cultural and public events in the Metaverse?

2 State of Art

2.1 The Metaverse: Echoing the Past

The emergence of the Internet and World Wide Web has fundamentally transformed how we communicate, learn, and disseminate information. However, computer-based communication predominantly remains static, still reliant on traditional tools like keyboards and monitors. Emerging modalities, such as multiparty video conferencing and large-scale collaborative virtual environments, have yet to fully replace more conventional methods like email due to inherent restrictions.

Cutting-edge innovations, like head-mounted virtual reality (VR) systems and see-through augmented reality (AR) displays, hold great promise and have begun to see more widespread adoption. These systems offer immersive experiences that far surpass the traditional PC and monitor interface but come with their own unique challenges. They can be notably difficult to install, configure, and maintain. Furthermore, these systems frequently necessitate specialized hardware and significant physical space, which restricts their usage largely to dedicated research facilities. As a result, their broader impact on the landscape of human-computer interaction remains limited.

Additionally, these immersive environments often operate as standalone systems and those supporting peer-to-peer communication necessitate high-bandwidth networks, which curtails their collaborative potential. Such communication is often feasible only between identical environments, further limiting the scope of collaboration and rendering these systems unsuitable for standard settings like offices or classrooms.

Addressing these challenges requires a multifaceted approach. Cost reduction, utilization of commodity parts, user-friendly design, and self-configuration capabilities are critical to make these systems a viable alternative for traditional office computing environments. Developing innovative communication models and efficient protocols for managing the Metaverse could significantly enhance the large-scale deployment and usage of these systems.

Interestingly, the notion of interoperability is a recurring theme in industry definitions, suggesting that a true Metaverse does not yet exist as it is absent in current virtual worlds. This raises questions about the conceptualization of the 'Metaverse' in academic discourse and its alignment with industry visions.

2.2 The Meta-stage: Presenting Future Stage

The Meta-stage emerged from a vision to bring virtual reality (VR) into theater experiences. The Meta-stage was conceptualized by a company collective – The White Hole Theater, who envisioned, designed and developed the Meta-stage. It was iteratively developed from basic motion capture and face-tracking technologies, ultimately incorporating fully-fledged VR environments replete with interactive game elements. In many respects, the Meta-stage mirrors past theater productions reported in research studies (Iudova-Romanova et al., 2023; Y.-C. N. Lee et al., 2013; J. Y. Park & Lim, 2022; Reaney, 1999) that explored the use of current and emerging computer technologies in theater production.

The aim is to explore how the concepts of engagement and immersion can be utilized to foster a connection between audiences and actors during live events. Metaverse-enabling technologies facilitate this connection, overcoming temporal and spatial separations. The VR theater context and technological infrastructure provided by the Meta-stage present an opportunity to examine the transferability and interoperability of such a setup. This investigation can contribute to the future vision of an interconnected Metaverse in various contexts and scenarios.

The primary goal of conventional VR technology in numerous applications is to replicate real-world scenes and conditions, with a focus on immersion. The commercial use of VR includes training pilots, ship captains, surgeons, and mechanics, prototyping new machines, and advancing architectural development. These applications typically aim for heightened realism to accurately simulate real-world scenarios.

While the Meta-stage does not aim for realism, it seeks to capitalize on immersion. It draws the audience into the play and enables interactions that facilitate an active participatory experience. This approach allows the audience to become co-creators with the actors, becoming part of the play or influencing the story that unfolds on the Meta-stage.

The early conceptual model for the Meta-stage (Fig. 1) is a physical stage where the actors wearing motion capture suits perform a live theatrical performance for the audience. The actors are rendered in a virtual environment, using a point cloud animation style, representing the avatars they enact. The audience can view the live performance traditionally from seating next to the stage and view the virtual content on large screen displays positioned around the stage at vantage points, or they can participate in virtual reality wearing head mounted displays, for a more immersed experience. Furthermore, the performance is live streamed, enabling audiences to view it from anywhere through both remote VR and 2D screens via virtual production setups.

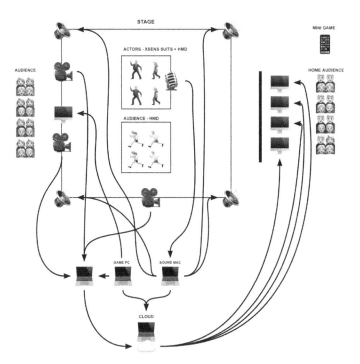

Fig. 1. The audience on both sides of the stage, with the actors (as purple emoji's) and the audience wearing VR HMD's (visualized as the running/active emojis)

2.3   The Meta-stage 'Tech Stack'

The current implementation of the Meta-stage consists of the following technical components:

- **Qualisys** (qualisys.com) provides precision motion capture and 3D positioning tracking systems that offer solutions for capturing and analyzing movements in sports, clinical science, biomechanics, animation, virtual reality, robotics, and more.
- **ARKit** (developer.apple.com/augmented-reality/arkit/), a framework developed by Apple, facilitates the creation of augmented reality experiences on iOS devices. It simplifies the task of building an AR experience. This is achieved by combining device motion tracking, camera scene capture, advanced scene processing, and display conveniences. It allows for the creation of many kinds of AR experiences using the front or rear camera of an iOS devices.
- **Xsens** (movella.com/products/xsens) is a supplier of 3D motion capture products, wearable sensors, and inertial sensors based on miniature MEMS inertial sensor technology.
- **Photon Engine** (photonengine.com) is a backend-as-a-service (BaaS) for multiplayer game development. It provides a global cross-platform multiplayer game backend for various platforms including Android, iOS, .NET, Mac OS, Unity 3D, Windows, Unreal Engine, and HTML5. This service is cloud-based, making it a scalable solution for game developers.

The diagram in Fig. 2 shows the tech stack for the current implementation of the Meta-stage.

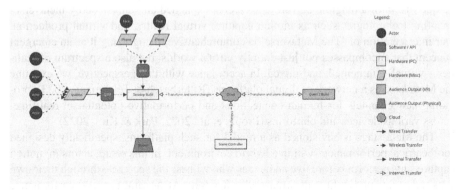

Fig. 2. The diagram illustrates the tech stack, comprising Qualisys, ARKit, and Photon Engine setup, combined with a physical stage

In future iterations, we intend to substitute the Qualisys system with OptiTrack (optitrack.com), an alternative high-performance optical motion tracking technology. Thus, in upcoming iterations of the VR performance 'The Battle,' audiences can participate in the live performances from various locations. This not only bridges the gap of physical distance but also enables interaction as if they were in the same location. This is made possible by the fusion of these technologies and the context that shapes the social interaction.

3   Concept Overview

In this paper, we present a case study of an ongoing live VR theater performance, "The Battle," which utilizes the Meta-stage to depict a historical event in medieval Denmark. This event was a battle, fought by three prospective kings of Denmark, which took place in Viborg in 1146. The victor of this battle would become the future king of Denmark and decide where the capitol of the country should be. The historical event is dramatized through a live re-enactment of the battle between the three aspiring kings. In addition to the Meta-stage physical stage and metaverse enabling technologies setup presented in previous subsections, the audience is given the opportunity to vote for the would-be king they believe should win the battle. This 'counterfactual' approach allows exploration of potential alternate histories that could have emerged had a different contender won the battle. As such, the play also incorporates elements of learning and reflection for the audience and integrates it through playful interaction where the audience are included into the play and allowed influence of the story's ending.

The Battle leverages Metaverse-enabling technologies to create a hybrid realm where virtual reality and the physical stage intersect. It is within this hybrid space that both audience and actors experience the Meta-stage performance—a form of hybrid co-presence, as it were.

Hybrid co-presence experiences, in this context, generally refer to the sensation of being together in the same place at the same time, a phenomenon often discussed in the realm of VR, AR, and online experiences where real-world and virtual interactions blend.

In this scholarly discourse, we introduce the novel concept of the 'Meta-stage'—a unique fusion of a tangible performance arena, expanded and enhanced by metaverse-enabling technologies such as motion capture, virtual reality, and virtual production. Our interpretation of 'The Metaverse' is comprehensive, recognizing it as an emergent concept that encompasses not just entirely virtual worlds, but also a spectrum of realities—virtual, augmented, and mixed. In accordance with this perspective, we examine the Metaverse as a network of digital platforms (Ritterbusch & Teichmann, 2023), providing new channels for human connections and performative potential in real-time, across various devices and platforms (Proulx et al., 2022; Park & Kim, 2022).

The Meta-stage is envisioned as a model for such platforms, specifically designed for theatrical performances within a hybrid environment. In this setup, actors in motion capture suits perform before live audiences who witness the spectacle through their own eyes and augmented reality via virtual reality headsets. At the same time, the performance is live streamed to remote audiences immersed in virtual reality environments. This setup allows audiences to become part of the performance through game-like interactions at key moments, thereby influencing various aspects of the live spectacle. Thus, the Meta-stage serves as a fusion of live non-digital performance, enhanced virtual reality motion capture performances, and far-reaching virtual reality experiences for remote audiences—all dynamically influenced by audience interaction.

We further illustrate the application of the Meta-stage through its use in three cultural heritage-themed theater performances in Denmark from 2021 to 2023. These performances creatively intertwine historical narratives from 1146 with contemporary scenarios, utilizing this hybrid performance approach (White Hole Theater, 2021).

3.1 Iterations of the Meta-stage

The current implementation of the Meta-stage and the performance, 'The Battle,' are part of an ongoing series of tests and developments, which started in 2021 and are projected to conclude in 2026. The Meta-stage performances started with smaller-scale setups and shows in 2021, where the system was conceptualized and built. Since then, the stage has been expanded and used for 'The Battle' in 2022, with 'The Battle 2' slated for performance in 2023.

The technical setup is subject to ongoing research and development, with new features like live streaming to audiences' homes and VR headset compatibility. These enhancements necessitate rigorous testing of both technical capacity and technological capability. The latter includes a close look at the resulting user experiences.

3.2 Iteration 1 – 'Arnolds Vision'

In June 2021, the production team, White Hole Theater, extended an invitation to audiences to traverse time and experience in Viborg and Stænderpladsen as it was in the year 1146, where the actual historical events took place. This immersive performance, named "Arnold's Vision", sought to provide a unique theatrical journey into a historical setting. Arnold's Vision was the first glimpse of the production, with a full launch planned for 2024. The event, stretching from sunset to sunrise, immersed participants in a night resplendent with spiritual encounters and prophetic visions (Fig. 3).

Fig. 3. Images from the test screening of 'Arnolds Vision'

The technological aspect of this experience hinged on the use of a VR headset, which transported participants 800 years back in time to the very spot they stood upon. An actor, adopting the persona of Arnold (a skjald), guided the audience (Lygtemanden) around the area, weaving tales about the place, its people, and the era. With the aid of a motion capture suit, the actor's movements were mirrored in the virtual world, thus breathing life into the character of Arnold in this immersive historical adventure. This first iteration consisted of motion tracking with Xsens, face tracking with ARKit and Photon Engine for the virtual reality environment and content.

3.3   Iteration 2 – 'The Battle 1'

Merging live performance and virtual reality, the first version of 'The Battle' was enacted by four actors donned in motion capture suits on an outdoor stage located in Stænder-pladsen, Viborg. These actors were supplemented by five extras, all outfitted with VR headsets. The movements of the actors were captured and transmitted to a server, which in turn controlled the actions of the main characters within a meticulously reconstructed 3D universe of Viborg, circa 1150. This reconstruction was carried out in partnership with the Viborg Museum and Denmark's premier medieval experts.

Like 'Arnold's Vision', a group of five audience members were invited to immerse themselves directly in the on-stage action. Equipped with VR headsets, these audience members took control of avatars, joining the fray either as part of 'Team Knud' or 'Team Valdemar', or playing the role of a monk assisting Bishop Svend with the Mass preceding the battle (Fig. 4).

Fig. 4. Images from scaled up tech stack being utilized for multiple VR audiences as well as live streams of 'The Battle 1'

The remaining audience could either witness the performance in person at the square or remotely via live streaming. Regardless of their location, all audience members had the capacity to influence the outcome of the performance. By sharing their perspectives through a Zoom link, they could actively participate in the battle for the Danish throne, thereby enhancing the immersive quality of this unique VR theater experience.

3.4   Iteration 3 – 'The Battle 2'

The forthcoming rendition of 'The Battle', scheduled for June 2023, will incorporate mini games, enabling audience participation throughout the performance. This addition aims to examine user agency within the performance and explore its influence on the interpretation of various outcomes, as well as on the immersion of both the on-stage and remote VR audiences.

This version also delves further into priming and orienting audiences to the narrative world and aesthetic visualizations. As demonstrated by previous research, inadequate orientation for first-time users of novel technological experiences can detrimentally impact the user experience (Vistisen et al., 2017). This is particularly significant with emerging technological experiences, where user expectations can be challenging to anticipate (Fig. 5).

Fig. 5. Images from 'The Battle 2' utilizing the new improved motion tracking in the tech stack as well as both a building-focused and a weapons-focused mini-game as part of the performance

This iteration builds upon the previous version of 'The Battle', featuring advancements in motion tracking and novel game elements designed to introduce audiences to the narrative world through interaction. Specifically, the mini games will engage VR audiences in mundane tasks, such as carrying wood, gathering weapons, and baking bread, facilitated by controllers with teleport movement. Furthermore, this iteration will be live-streamed, enabling remote audiences to participate from various locations.

3.5   Iteration 4 – 'Three Kings'

'The Battle 1' and 'The Battle 2' represent the initial parts of White Hole Theatre's epic drama 'Three Kings'. The insights gathered from the three preceding iterations will inform a minor iteration in 2024, aptly named 'Valdemar's Story', which will pave the way for the final production, 'Three Kings', scheduled for 2026. In this final performance, the boundaries between audience members, the physical stage, and the Meta-stage will be thoroughly explored and tested. This process aims to gauge the potential of future digital theatre formats by leveraging the accumulated experiences from the entire tech stack.

4   Perspectives/Discussion

4.1   Reflecting on the Meta-Stage Iterations

The Meta-stage has thus far affirmed the potential of contemporary metaverse-enabling technologies in crafting immersive and engaging narratives. However, a thorough evaluation of the resultant user experiences and the distinct impacts of different elements within the technology stack is yet to be undertaken. The incorporation of game design to stimulate active audience participation through interaction is a promising approach, but the implications of such engagement on user experience remain largely unexplored. The Meta-stage's past iterations have showcased a systematic integration and refinement of technical facets through performances, culminating in a level of maturity conducive to user testing. This progression sets the stage for a more detailed examination of user experiences in relation to the technologies employed. Such an analysis is crucial for understanding the realm of possibilities before addressing broader questions, such as the transferability to other contexts and interoperability, which are essential steps towards a unified metaverse.

4.2   The User Experiences

This study has mapped out the tech stack that enables the Meta-stage – a combination of metaverse enabling technologies that are utilized to create a live performance on a hybrid stage. Through the four iterations the common motivation has been to understand the current state of the potential of the Meta-stage both conceptually and in practice. In order to fully develop a perspective on this, the next step is to study the resulting real life user experiences from a hybrid stage setup that invites audiences to view the performance as a theater show and encourages them to step into a fully immersed virtual reality where they can experience the theater performance as a part of the gathering of townsfolk that witnessed the events of the battle of the three kings.

The Battle 2 performed in 2023 is a steppingstone towards the fourth larger scale iteration 'Three Kings' in 2026. Therefore, it is important to understand the user experiences so that they may inform future iterations of the planned production in terms of interactive elements as well as the technical setup.

We will focus future studies on evaluating the user experience of the audience present at the physical stage – both with and without VR headsets, and the audiences that are tele present via live stream.

In essence, the objective is to conduct a feasibility study to ascertain audience perceptions of the experience, using these insights to inform future iterations for the 2024 and 2026 shows. As previously mentioned, we aim to examine transferability and interoperability by understanding the resulting user experiences. These insights will contribute to shaping the future of the metaverse and its potential applications.

4.3   A Meta-stage for Transferability and Interoperability in the Metaverse?

The term "metaverse" is continually evolving due to ongoing technical and technological advancements. These progressions persistently alter the landscape of potential interactions, communications, and collaborations within the metaverse. With the recent surge in media attention, the metaverse has captivated the collective consciousness of researchers, industry professionals, and the general public alike, making it a fascinating research focus.

This study aims to report on a specially built stage designed for cultural contexts, specifically live stage theater performances. However, the broader ambition is to gain insights about the possibilities, limitations, implications, and challenges that need to be addressed in the near future while also envisioning the distant future of the metaverse. The immediate focus is on how studies around the user experiences of the Meta-stage can inform future iterations of the Meta-stage and benefit other similar contexts, such as public events.

Long-term considerations relate to the question of interoperability within the metaverse. This involves exploring how entities within the metaverse can conform to a protocol that ensures an open, decentralized and interoperable metaverse.

5 Conclusion

This study presents a novel conceptualization of the metaverse, the Meta-stage, which integrates a range of metaverse-enabling technologies. The ongoing development of the Meta-stage has reached a stage of maturity where user testing is beneficial for investigating the user experiences that emerge from interactions within the Meta-stage.

His approach offers a unique interpretation of the metaverse, potentially providing insights into how to develop and enhance metaverse interactions. Such insights could contribute to the formulation of design guidelines for cultural and public events that take advantage of metaverse and metaverse-enabling technologies, thereby enabling the transfer of knowledge to other contexts. Furthermore, the future trajectory of the Meta-stage and research conducted within this framework could yield valuable knowledge to inform the broader development of the metaverse.

References

Almoqbel, M.Y., Naderi, A., Wohn, D.Y., Goyal, N.: The metaverse: a systematic literature review to map scholarly definitions. In: Companion Publication of the 2022 Conference on Computer Supported Cooperative Work and Social Computing, pp. 80–84 (2022). 10/gr9dh2

Benedikt, M.L.: Cityspace, cyberspace, and the spatiology of information. J. Virtual Worlds Res. 1(1) (2008). 10/gr9dhz

Dixon, S.: A history of virtual reality in performance. Int. J. Perform. Arts Digit. Media 2(1), 23–54 (2006). 10/fjtqfz

Iudova-Romanova, K., Humenyuk, T., Horevalov, S., Honcharuk, S., Mykhalov, V.: Virtual reality in contemporary theatre. J. Comput. Cult. Heritage 15(4), 75:1–75:11 (2023). 10/gr9dh7

Jernigan, D., Fernandez, S., Pensyl, R., Shangping, L.: Digitally augmented reality characters in live theatre performances. Int. J. Perform. Arts Digit. Media 5(1), 35–49 (2009). 10/c3wzk8

Kraus, S., Kanbach, D.K., Krysta, P.M., Steinhoff, M.M., Tomini, N.: Facebook and the creation of the metaverse: radical business model innovation or incremental transformation? Int. J. Entrep. Behav. Res. 28(9), Article 9 (2022). 10/gqfbhf

Lee, L.-H., et al.: All One Needs to Know about Metaverse: A Complete Survey on Technological Singularity, Virtual Ecosystem, and Research Agenda (arXiv:2110.05352) (2021). arXiv. http://arxiv.org/abs/2110.05352

Lee, Y.-C., Shan, L.-T., Chen, C.-H.: System development of immersive technology theatre in museum. In: Shumaker, R. (ed.) VAMR 2013. LNCS, vol. 8022, pp. 400–408. Springer, Heidelberg (2013). https://doi.org/10.1007/978-3-642-39420-1_42

Metaverse Standards Forum. The Metaverse Standards Forum. Metaverse Standards Forum (2022). https://metaverse-standards.org/

Mystakidis, S.: Metaverse. Encyclopedia **2**(1), 486–497 (2022). 10/hsfw

Narin, N.G.: A content analysis of the metaverse articles. J. Metaverse **1**(1), 17–24 (2021)

Park, J.Y., Lim, Y.K.: Metaverse-driven interactive performing arts content development. In: Stephanidis, C., Antona, M., Ntoa, S., Salvendy, G. (eds.) HCII 2022. CCIS, vol. 1654, pp. 329–335. Springer, Cham (2022). https://doi.org/10.1007/978-3-031-19679-9_41

Park, S.-M., Kim, Y.-G.: A metaverse: taxonomy, components, applications, and open challenges. IEEE Access **10**, 4209–4251 (2022). 10/grmjq3

Radoff, J.: The Metaverse Value-Chain. Building the Metaverse (2021). https://medium.com/building-the-metaverse/the-metaverse-value-chain

Reaney, M.: Virtual reality and the theatre: immersion in virtual worlds. Digit. Creativity **10**(3), 183–188 (1999). 10/fj6wq7

Ritterbusch, G.D., Teichmann, M.R.: Defining the metaverse: a systematic literature review. IEEE Access **11**, 12368–12377 (2023). 10/gr9dh9

Rospigliosi, P.A.: Metaverse or Simulacra? Roblox, Minecraft, Meta and the turn to virtual reality for education, socialisation and work. Interact. Learn. Environ. **30**(1), Article 1 (2022). 10/gr6s6d

Sargeant, B.: PluginHUMAN - Immersive Art. PluginHUMAN (2013). https://pluginhuman.com/

Simpson, J., Foster, R.: Liveness for Contemporary Audiences: Developing online-togetherness in metaverse theatre audiences (2022). 10/gr9dh4

Stephenson, N.: Snow Crash. Bantam Books (1992)

Vistisen, P., Østergaard, C.P., Krishnasamy, R.K.: Adopting the unknown through the known: supporting user interaction of non-idiomatic technologies in exhibitions through known idioms of conventional technologies. Des. J. Eur. Acad. Des. **20**, S3696–S3706 (2017). 10/ghzc7v

Wang, Y., et al.: A Survey on Metaverse: Fundamentals, Security, and Privacy (arXiv:2203.02662; Issue arXiv:2203.02662) (2022). arXiv. https://doi.org/10.48550/arXiv.2203.02662

White Hole Theater. 3 Kings. WHITE HOLE THEATER (2021). https://www.whiteholetheater.dk/projects

Zyda, M.: Let's rename everything "the metaverse!" Computer **55**(3), 124–129 (2022). 10/grt895

Gamifying the Museum: Enhancing Immersive Art Experiences with Social Connections and Personal Identity Exploration

Atakan Akcali[(⊠)] [iD]

Teesside University, Tees Valley, Middlesbrough TS1 3BX, UK
a.akcali@tees.ac.uk

Abstract. This paper explores how social and gamified museum experiences can enhance the immersive art experience, encouraging engagement and interactivity. Museums provide a safe space for visitors to explore their individual identities and connect with others, forging personal connections and shared experiences. People often visit museums with friends or family to spend quality time together. Social and gamified immersive art experiences provide interactive environments that challenge assumptions and facilitate meaningful interactions, allowing individuals to explore their identities and develop a sense of belonging. By harnessing the transformative power of games and immersive art, individuals navigate the complexities of their identities, fostering understanding and connection within themselves and their community. Many museums now offer exhibits that encourage active participation, immersing visitors in different worlds and creating unique, unforgettable experiences. This study reveals that visitors primarily seek to appreciate art, gain knowledge, inspiration, creativity, and positive emotions like happiness and warmth. Participants expressed interest in gamified experiences and forming new connections. These findings can guide museums in tailoring their programs to meet visitors' needs and desires. By utilising these findings, museums can acquire significant knowledge and enhance their programs to cater to the requirements and desires of their visitors more effectively.

Keywords: Social and Gamified Experiences · Museum Experiences · Social Interactions · Role-Playing · Immersive Art · Identity Exploration

1 Introduction

Visitors accept museums as physical spaces where the latest technology can be experienced [1]. With the nascent usage of digital technologies, museums have been gaining the potential to offer more for their visitors than a traditional museum visitation experience. Museums also provide safe environments for visitors to construct and explore their identities; according to Rounds [2], a museum visit involves both the creation of identity and the signalling of identity; being somebody is good, but it's even better to be someone else every once in a while, and museums provide chances to affirm our current identities and safely investigate alternatives.

© ICST Institute for Computer Sciences, Social Informatics and Telecommunications Engineering 2024
Published by Springer Nature Switzerland AG 2024. All Rights Reserved
D. Crawford et al. (Eds.): TIE 2023, LNICST 575, pp. 107–123, 2024.
https://doi.org/10.1007/978-3-031-59383-3_8

The International Council of Museums defines museums as welcoming and inclusive to the public, promoting diversity and sustainability, and conducting their operations with ethics and professionalism while involving communities in their activities and offering a wide range of experiences that are intended to educate, entertain, and provide opportunities for reflection and knowledge-sharing [3]. Being in the museum space is important because it provides a place for constructing meaning, immersing oneself in the museum context, and engaging in social interactions that contribute to personal connections and shared experiences. Museums hold a social dimension as visitors are most likely to go to museums with others [4], and one of their primary motivations for visiting is to spend time with friends or family [5, 6]. Moreover, Benjamin [7] claims that even the most faithful reproduction of a work of art cannot capture its unique existence in a specific time and place, which is marked by the history and changes it has undergone in terms of physical structure and ownership. The place is a centre of meaning, and it is constructed by experience; also, the sense of place and experiencing the place require time, and often it does not happen incidentally [8]. Johnston [9] describes places as being experimental rather than physical, and places have indispensable features of character, identity, and "spirit". As an already social area, the museum experience supported by the opportunities of immersive experiences can fortify new or existing relationships, just as Huizinga claims, stating that "a play community generally tends to become permanent even after the game is over" [10].

Museums have been known to use digital technologies for several reasons, such as improving the experience and education, elongating time spent and increasing engagement and visitation frequencies. Audio guides are the traditional way of engaging with the modern museum experience and having an audio tour for most museums has become a must [11]. These tours mainly provide information and lead the visitors through the museum and exhibitions [12]. While some museums offer their own devices, others ask visitors to use their personal mobile phones. Moreover, podcasts are utilised to give detailed information about the museum objects or discuss the collection with their guests [13, 14]. Besides informing their guests about the exhibitions, some museums embark on creative approaches such as incorporating music to deepen the experience and add sensory reinforcement to specific collections by creating relevant playlists [15, 16].

The shift towards the visitor's role as an engaged participant rather than a mere spectator has led to an increase in the use and popularity of immersive exhibit forms [17]. Immersive technologies give visitors a distinct experience by transporting them to a different world [18]. Exhibits that assign a specific role to visitors tend to have a higher level of immersion, as visitors can play a role, such as rabbits in an underground burrow with interconnected tunnels and peepholes to view an aboveground rabbit exhibit [17]. Both museum visits and play offer individuals a sense of freedom from everyday lives. Visitors can temporarily escape their daily routines and immerse themselves in the exhibits in museums. Likewise, play provides an opportunity to step out of everyday lives and enter a space where rules and boundaries may differ, allowing for greater freedom of expression, creativity, and exploration. The need for play is an instinctual act of leisure freedom, only remains compelling at the extent of the entertainment it provides and can be stopped at any time as it is "never a task," but rather a voluntary act of stepping out of real-life [10]. Impersonating alternate and imaginary roles, therefore, may enhance the art experience. 1944 Warsaw Rising Museum's interactive museum experience 'Reflection. I am like you, I daresay' allows visitors to match and impersonate historical characters from the museum's archives, and visitors are encouraged to question their identity and their individual fates in this collective experience while experiencing the exhibit from someone else's eyes [19]. According to Bowman [20], humans perceive themselves as independent beings without the need for others' opinions and expectations, yet their brains seek recognition, endorsement, and integration with others, allowing them to adopt various identities to match social and environmental conditions and shift between them without much deliberation, which is why identity alteration in role-playing games provides the opportunity to experience different roles in "low consequence" settings. Museum objects can strengthen personal identity and belonging; furthermore, the essential values of a sound community which are collective meaning, sharing, discussion and debate, can be experienced through museum objects [21]. An identity is differentiated by what it is not and marked out by unlikeness; also, focusing on difference involves a denial that there are similarities [22]. However, games allow people to enter a magic circle in which they can freely negotiate boundaries around predetermined attachments and beliefs [23]. Therefore, social and gamified immersive art experiences could offer a distinct opportunity for individuals to delve into and reconcile their personal identities while fostering a sense of belonging. By creating a playful and interactive environment, these experiences allow participants to transcend traditional boundaries, challenge preconceived notions, and engage in collective meaning-making, sharing, discussion, and debate. Through the transformative power of games and immersive art, individuals can navigate the complexities of identity and difference, fostering a deeper understanding and connection within themselves and the larger community.

Based on the study of Smith, Smith and Tinio, visitor profiles based on group size can be categorised into three groups: alone, two people and three to six people, and behaviour towards artwork varies correspondingly [24]. The study found that the mean time spent looking at art is 17.94 s for a single visitor, whilst it is 21.41 for two people and 25.07 for a group of visitors from three to six. The study also found that the mean time spent reading the artwork labels is 8.88 s for a single visitor, 8.37 for two people and 7.40 for a group of visitors from three to six. The total amount spent on an artwork combining both the view of the artwork itself and reading the label is 28.82 for a single visitor, 29.79 for two people and 32.46 for a group of visitors from three to six. To fortify the effect of this organic phenomenon which occurs when people visit museums in groups, several museums are also creating intentional strategies to extend museum visits, such as the *slow museum visit*. This way of visiting encourages visitors to take their time and allow themselves to make personal connections with the artworks [25]. The Rubin Museum also encourages this mindful approach pointing out that it could provide rewarding experiences in museums and galleries for years to come [26].

The growing mobile gaming industry and its expanding usage have also shown their presence in museums and cultural institutions. Mobile games provide some advantages, such as lower production costs, fast and easy downloads, being casual and accessible, and, most significantly, allowing for portability [27]. *Sofias Smuggling, cross–border hunt*, is a mobile app that combines eight thematically different museums through gameplay. In this game, users are asked to collect digital objects and solve mini-games related to the museums' exhibitions [28]. Whilst *Sofias Smuggling* is aimed towards a younger audience, other concepts' primary focus is adult audiences. The mobile application concept Acht suggests an experience shaped around dating and socialising in museums that also contains gamified features provided by some mini-games helping its users to get acquainted with each other [29]. As evidence supporting the usage of mobile phones in museums, the study by Smith et al. found that with the widespread use of mobile phones, 35% of their sample group took selfies with the artworks [24]. Likewise, including social layers to a museum visit supported by digital technologies can provide an additional experience similar to the benefit of digital services.

Museums utilise technology to enhance visitors' experiences and enable them to explore their identities in a secure environment. These public, diverse, and ethical institutions offer a distinctive sense of character and identity. By providing immersive experiences, visitors can create meaning and engage in social interactions that foster relationships. Digital technology is utilised to enhance these experiences. With activities like role-playing, museums can further immerse visitors in the experience and promote personal identity. Playful art experiences offer a sense of freedom and belonging, allowing individuals to navigate complex identities and connect with their community. Therefore, incorporating social and gamified experiences can enhance the overall museum experience.

2   Methodology

This research employed a mixed-methods approach, combining a self-administered survey administered to a wide range of participants and interviews conducted with museum professionals. The survey aimed to understand the participants' frequency of museum visits, frequency of playing games and opinions on and behaviours during a museum visit. The interviews aimed to investigate the views and concerns of museum professionals from different areas of expertise on visitor behaviour, socialising, and gamified museum experiences.

2.1   Data Collection

The data collection for the survey was performed in a self-administered fashion using Google Forms. The sample size was 654 participants. The data were collected anonymously from February 8 to March 24, 2021, and participants were made aware that they could choose not to submit their responses if they were uncomfortable with any part of the survey, but if they did submit the survey, they provided consent to participate in this research. The survey consisted of 13 questions, including a five-point Likert scale, radio buttons and checkboxes, and an open-text option for those who wished to add their opinion. The survey contained seven sections in total. Since there was a key question, respondents would follow different paths throughout the survey. The first section had two demographic questions, and the second section focused on the participants' museum visiting and game-playing frequencies. The third section was only for participants who responded, as *I don't visit museums* that were then directed to section six. Participants who chose answers other than *I don't visit museums* continued the fourth section. This section was comprised of two questions that focused mainly on engagement. Section five focused on understanding the primary motivation for museum visits and the participants' perception of museums. Section six was the main section covering two questions on making new friends and playing games at museums. The last section, section seven, contained one question asking what the participants wanted to take away from the museum at the end of their visit.

The interviews focused on investigating the opinions and concerns of museum professionals from different areas of expertise on visitor behaviour, socialising, and gamified museum experiences. Eleven interviewees from Germany, Turkey and the United Kingdom were selected from various positions: Director of Learning, Education Assistant, Collections and Learning Curator, Senior Engagement Officer, Scientific Associate, Tour Guide, Head of Digital Engagement, and Digital Producer. Participants were informed that they could choose not to submit their answers if they felt uncomfortable with any part of the interview. The interviewees were informed that they were being recorded. They were also informed that by participating in the interview or replying via email, they indicated that they provided consent to participate in this research. The video interviews started with reading the consent text, and the email interviews included a consent text. During the transcriptions identities of the interviewees were made anonymous. The interview was five to six questions long, depending on the interviewees' professions. Interviewees were offered the choice of either a video interview or an email interview. The interviews took place in February and April of 2021, and the majority of participants opted to respond via email due to scheduling conflicts. Questions were slightly adapted to suit interviewees' professions in museums while keeping the main structure of the interview.

2.2 Museum Visiting Survey Analysis

The following presents the results of a comprehensive survey conducted to explore various aspects of museum visitation and visitor experiences. With a sample size of 654 participants, the survey aimed to uncover insights regarding visitor demographics, frequency of museum visits, motivations for visiting, engagement with exhibits, definition and expectations of museums, desires and takeaways from museum visits, as well as experiences of playing games and making new friends within museum settings. The findings provide valuable data and perspectives that contribute to a deeper understanding of visitor behaviours and preferences, offering insights that can inform the development of more engaging and tailored museum experiences. There are two main age groups, as 45% (n: 294) of the participants ages are between 18–24, and the other 45% (n: 294) are between 25–34. The frequency of visits to museums in the duration of a year, 34% (n: 220) of the participants visit *rarely*, 24% (n: 154) of participants visit *sometimes,* and 21% (n: 136) visit *occasionally.* 10% (n: 65) of the participants visit *often,* while 4% visit *regularly.* 8% (n: 52) of the participants answered that they *do not visit museums at all.* This data shows that respondents *occasionally* visit museums ($M = 3.94$, $SD = 1.29$). Only 8% of the participants answered that they do not go to museums, and the main reason provided is that they do not have motivation ($M = 3.69$, $SD = 1.32$). The secondary reasons are that they don't have time ($M = 3.31$, $SD = 1.29$), that they find museums boring ($M = 3.15$, $SD = 1.43$) and that they get tired ($M = 3.06$, $SD = 1.32$).

The survey asked participants' frequency of playing games (board, mobile, card etc.) (n: 654) and 30% (n: 191) answered *regularly*, 23% (n: 150) *sometimes*, 22% (n: 143) *often*, 12% (n: 77) *rarely*, 9% (n: 61) *occasionally* and 5% (n: 32) reported they *do not play games at all.* Hence, the respondents *sometimes* play games ($M = 2.67, SD = 1.51$) (see Fig. 1).

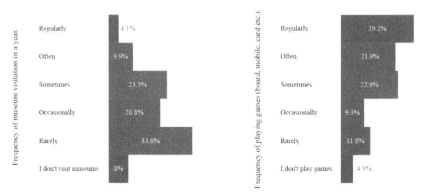

Fig. 1. The frequency of visits to museums in the duration of a year and frequency of playing games (board, mobile, card etc.)

In line with the previous studies, the overwhelming majority (85%) of people surveyed responded that they do not visit museums alone. 70% of the respondents visit museums with a friend/s (n: 421), 46% (n: 278) visit with family, 46% (n: 277) visit with a partner, date or spouse, 33% (n: 196) visit alone and 26% (n: 156) with school or university (see Fig. 2).

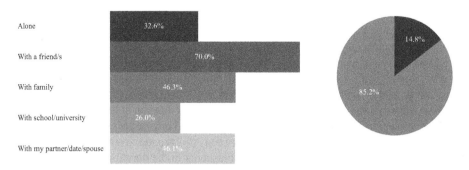

Fig. 2. Museum Visitors' Accompaniment Preferences

Museum visitors have diverse reasons for visiting museums. The largest portion of respondents, 77% of cases (n: 459), visit museums as a touristic activity or day trip visit. The second largest portion, 75% (n: 448), visit museums for education and learning. 66% (n: 393) go for entertainment, and 59% (n: 356) for enjoyment. 58% (n: 346) visit museums for a specific artwork or exhibition, and 48% (n: 290) visit to experience the past. 41% (n: 248) go to museums to spend some time with friend/s, whilst 33% (n: 196) visit for an event, activity or workshop. 31% (n: 186) visit museums as something to do in their spare time (see Fig. 3).

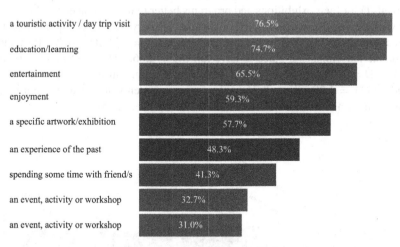

Fig. 3. Reasons for Museum Visits

The survey included a question aimed at gaining a better understanding of the diverse ways in which museum visitors engage with the exhibits. Predictably, the respondents are most likely to look at the artworks and exhibitions ($M = 4.69$, $SD = 0.71$). The vast majority also reads labels ($M = 4.36$, $SD = 0.85$), and if they are with a companion/s, they exchange ideas about the artworks and exhibitions ($M = 3.90$, $SD = 1.16$). Respondents also take photos of the artworks and exhibitions ($M = 3.52$, $SD = 1.3$) and check online sources about the artworks ($M = 3.03$, $SD = 1.31$) (see Fig. 4).

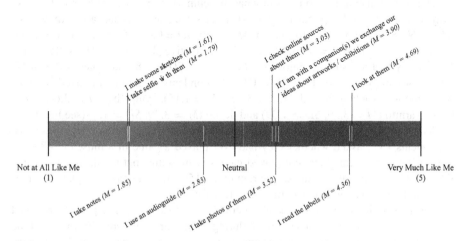

Fig. 4. Engagement with Museum Exhibits

It's important to note that the definition of museums can vary from person to person, as individuals may have different reasons for visiting museums and engaging with their exhibits. Therefore, asking participants to define what a museum means to them can provide valuable insights into their motivations and expectations and help museum professionals tailor their exhibitions and programs better to meet the needs and interests of their visitors. The overwhelming majority of people surveyed have responded that they define museums as seeing artworks and exhibitions (M = 4.53 SD = 0.78). Respondents also define museums as a place to have fun (M = 3.86, SD = 0.98) and to relax (M = 3.52, SD = 1.12). However, respondents do not define museums as places only kids would go (M = 1.39, SD = 0.71). Likewise, respondents do not define museums as places to make new friends (M = 1.76, SD = 0.91) (see Fig. 5).

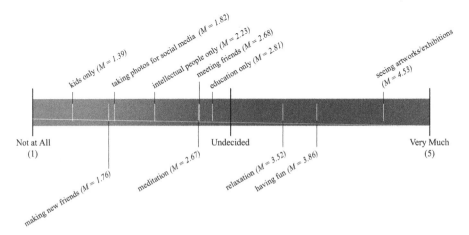

Fig. 5. Definition of Museums Among Visitors

The survey also aimed to explore what museum visitors desire and expect to take away from their visit. Respondents (n: 654) have a strong desire to take away knowledge ($M = 4.60, SD = 0.65$) and information ($M = 4.56, SD = 0.64$). They also have a strong desire to feel inspired ($M = 4.43, SD = 0.83$) and creative ($M = 4.37, SD = 0.85$) whilst taking away feelings such as enjoyment ($M = 4.30, SD = 0.8$), happiness ($M = 4.15, SD = 0.86$) and fun ($M = 4.02, SD = 0.9$). Respondents wish to feel relaxed and take away emotions such as empathy ($M = 3.64, SD = 1.15$), sympathy ($M = 3.64, SD = 1.06$), warmth ($M = 3.59, SD = 1.09$) and desire ($M = 3.39, SD = 1.2$) (see Fig. 6).

As part of the survey aimed at understanding visitors' engagement with museums, respondents were asked whether they had ever played a game in a museum. 48% (n: 313) of the respondents have not played games in museums but would like to, whilst 37% (n: 240) have played games. The remaining 15% (n: 101) have not played games and do not wish to play games in museums (see Fig. 7).

To gain insight into visitors' social experiences at museums, participants were asked whether they had ever made a new friend during a museum visit. Only 7% (n: 46) of the respondents have made friends in museums. An overwhelming majority of respondents,

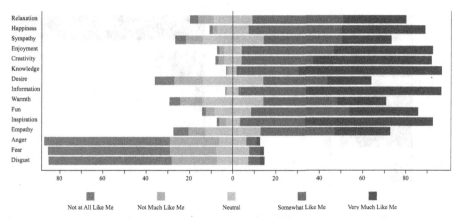

Fig. 6. Visitor Desires and Expectations from Museum Visits

71% (n: 463), have not made friends but would like to. 22% (n: 145) of respondents have not made friends and would not like to (see Fig. 7).

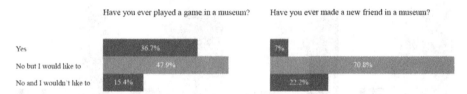

Fig. 7. Visitors' Engagement and Openness in Playing Games and Formation of New Friendships in Museums

The following data analyses the relationship between (n: 602) who *do not at all define museums as a place to make new friends* with *whether or not they have ever made a new friend in a museum* (see Fig. 8). 17% (n: 8) of the respondents who have made a new friend in a museum do *not at all* define museums as a place to make new friends, 45% (n: 196) of the respondents who have not but would like to make a new friend in a museum and 75% (n: 92) of the respondents who have not and would not like to make a new friend in a museum do *not at all* define museums as a place to make new friends. Only 9% (n: 4) of the respondents who have made a new friend in a museum *very much* define museums as a place to make new friends, and 1% (n: 4) of them have not but would like to make a new friend in a museum. 95% of the respondents who have not and would not like to make new friends in museums do not define museums as a place to make new friends. On the contrary, 82% of the respondents who have not but would like to make new friends in museums do not define museums for making new friends (see Fig. 8).

Based on the survey results, the majority of the respondents who visit a museum for *entertainment, spending some time with friend/s, enjoyment* or *a touristic activity/day trip* have either played a game in a museum or would like to play a game in a museum see Fig. 9).

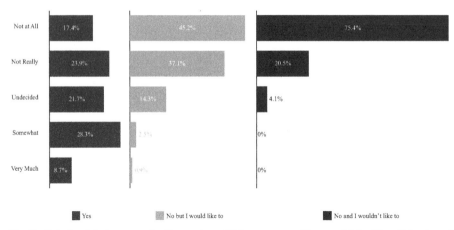

Fig. 8. Relationship between the Perception of Museums as a Place to Make New Friends and Previous Friend-Making Experiences in Museums.

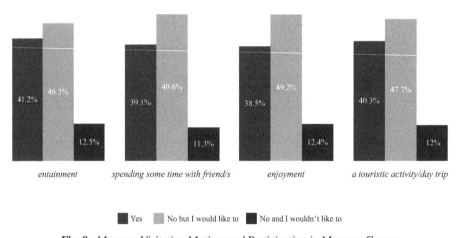

Fig. 9. Museum Visitation Motives and Participation in Museum Games

It is also clear that the vast majority of the respondents who visit a museum for *entertainment, spending some time with friend/s, enjoyment* or *a touristic activity/day trip* have either made a new friend in a museum or would like to make a new friend in a museum (see Fig. 10).

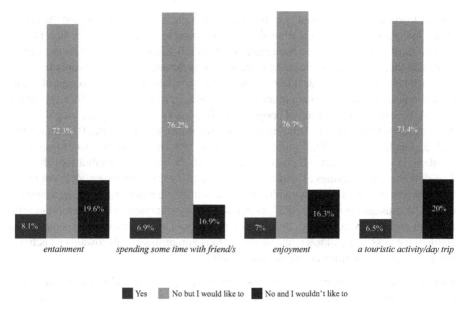

Yes   No but I would like to   No and I wouldn't like to

Fig. 10. Relationship between Museum Visitation Motives and Making New Friends

2.3 Experts Interview Analysis

This section presents a series of expert interviews conducted with museum profession-als to gain insights into visitors' engagement, motivations, behaviours, and museum experiences. The interviews covered various topics, including personal definitions of a museum, visitors' primary motivations for visiting, interactions with artworks and exhibitions, the role of games and play in museums, desired takeaways for visitors, and observations on socialising in museums. These questions aim to provide a deeper understanding of how museum professionals perceive and approach visitor engagement and how they envision the role of museums in contemporary society. Thematic analysis, as defined by Braun and Clarke [30], was employed to identify and analyse patterns within the data using a data-driven and inductive approach. The software Quirkos was utilised for analysing the interview transcripts. While the survey gathered information from visitors, the expert interviews helped to identify themes such as acceptance within limitations, engagement, museum properties, museum output, and visitor behaviours.

Acceptance within Limitations. Data extracts such as: "noisy without difficulties", "collectiveness and individuality", and "being very quiet" have been coded as *visitor behaviour* in museums, and that code has been mentioned 12 times. "They are welcome to respond as they see fit", "I would love to see a group of adult people having fun", and "feeling comfortable to be themselves" are some examples of data extracts coded as *museum acceptance of visitor freedom*. This code has been mentioned 14 times through-out the interviews. The code *behaviour, engagement and security limitations* introduced by the museum and that code has been mentioned 17 times and includes data extracts such as "unless they are doing anything dangerous, or that upsets other visitors", "as long as there are no guests that may be disturbed in the immediate area" and "wardens of the museum". The aforementioned codes combine to create the theme acceptance without limitations which have been mentioned overall 43 times. The *acceptance within limitation* theme describes museum professionals' welcoming manner towards freedom of visitor behaviour as long as it remains within the limitations of the museum rules and regulations whilst not disturbing other visitors or museum content. Therefore, making it possible to assume that a group of people socialising and participating in a playful activity in a museum atmosphere will be tolerated. According to Interviewee 03, behaviours such as laughing and making noise indicating visitors are having fun would not be a problem, in contrast to actions such as running, which might cause vibrations that can disturb the sensitive casings of artworks. In accordance with Interviewee 04, it would not be a problem as long as visitor conduct remains within the realms of safety and care for others. "A museum is not a temple", as pointed out by Interviewee 05, consolidates the freedom encouraged to visitors by museum professionals. These examples support the claim of the possibility of tolerance shown by museum professionals towards an activity when museum limitations are taken into account.

Engagement. The data extracts, "interactives and programming", "virtual reality chariot race", and "AR technologies", are a few examples that have been coded as *digital technology used in museums that visitors may interact with,* and that code has been mentioned 9 times. "Looking at objects in cases", "wander around on their own", "take pictures", "take notes", and "go around quickly and focus on what they really want to see" are data extracts that have been coded as *the manner in which visitors engage with museum content* and that code has been mentioned 46 times. These two codes combined form the theme *engagement* that has been mentioned as a sum total of 55 times. The theme *engagement* is constructed from two codes; the first being one of its components, digital engagement methods used by museums and the second defining the fashion in which visitors choose to experience museum content. It may be achievable to point out that even though museums provide a certain type of engagement, visitors may choose to engage in a preferred personal manner. According to Interviewee 04, some visitors prefer to play with the interactives, while others spend more time comprehending content through labels. According to Interviewee 03, some visitors "go around the Gallery and explore in your (their) own time". Interviewee 02 describes the opportunity to hold an original artefact as an engagement type. In contrast, Interviewee 06 states that there is an "indescribable desire in people to touch the artworks". "Silent tour between your mind and some imagery around you" is the way Interviewee 09 describes museum engagement, and for Interviewee 05, museum engagement enables "(visitors) to develop their own story". From the standpoint of these statements, visitor engagement preference may vary independently from museum-provided content.

Museum Properties. Data extracts such as "wellbeing programme for carers", "children's craft or storytelling activities", "LGBT tours", "black history tours", "educational programs", and "yoga" have been coded *as activities done in the museum and or hosted by the museum* such as *tours, seminars, workshops and events* and that code has been mentioned 34 times. "Science content", "historic properties", "archaeology", and "art" are some examples of data extracts coded as *museum and exhibition content*. This code has been mentioned 31 times. The code *facilities, properties and services specific to* *the museum* that has been mentioned 23 times consists of data extracts such as "good facilities (café, toilets, baby changing)", "tearoom", "safe indoor space", "the shop and the café", "neoclassical architecture with surrounding park" and "location". The data extracts that make up the code *admission fees existing or not* have been mentioned 6 times. These codes combined form the theme *museum properties* that has been mentioned a total of 94 times. The *museum properties* theme is composed of different elements that are provided by or presented in museums, albeit physical properties such as facilities, services and cost, museum content like; permanent or temporary exhibitions and activities arranged or hosted by the museum, such as workshops, seminars and events. This theme provides useful information on the correlational data between museum properties and visitor behaviour, motivations for visiting and activities done in museums. In accordance with Interviewee 03, there are various museum activities such as escape rooms, sleepovers, and tours hosted by the museum that permit visitors to explore different areas of the castle that self-admitted visitors cannot go to. According to Interviewee 07, there are more interactive offers specifically designed for families with children. Interviewee 06 states that their museum location also offers enjoyment of a nice view, solidifying the options of various museum facilities' attractions as visitation motivations. These examples provide different aspects of museum properties and the effects of these properties on visitor preferences.

Museum Output. Data extracts such as "fun, or to feel excited and happy", "calm", "feel comfortable", "fascinated by something", and "entertained" have been mentioned 33 times and coded as *fun centred emotional experience* whilst data extracts such as "to argue", "to change your mindset or your views" and "asking more questions" have been coded as *challenging, thought-provoking and expanding of one's views* and that code has been mentioned 14 times. "Leave wanting to find out more", "eager to hear", and "curiosity" are some of the term examples coded as *wanting to know more about museum content,* and that code has been mentioned 10 times. The code *getting inspired, learning, and expanding on something* has been mentioned 59 times and includes data extracts such as "to feel stimulated", "contextual and practical information", "their spirits stirred", "inspired to learn more", "to be socially educated", "empathy", "sense of discovery", "new idea and new experience". Data extracts such as "suitable for all ages and abilities", "represent and reflect the communities", and "there is something for them in museums" have been mentioned 15 times and coded as *the feeling of everyone being welcome in museums.* The data extracts that build the code *feeling satisfied, accomplished, and fulfilled* have been mentioned 4 times. The combination of these data extracts forms the theme *museum output* that has been mentioned a total of 140 times. The *museum output* theme resides in emotional, informative, and experiential outcomes that museum professionals aspire visitors to experience during or after a museum visit. The following statements point out how museum professionals define museums and, parallel to their definitions, what type of experiences they want visitors to take away. Interviewee 04 noted that museum professionals wish for visitors to think about the past, present and future and where they sit within it. Interviewee 03 states, "I'm quite happy for visitors to come to us and go away had not remembering (*sic*) any facts that they've learned, but perhaps wanting to find out more". In accordance with Interviewee 01 and Interviewee 05, understanding an artist's approach to the world and exploring their vision, in addition to the expansion of knowledge or ideas, are different possible conclusions from a museum visit. The inclusive aim of Interviewee 02 is for anyone from every part of society to feel welcome. These examples reinforce the parallelism between museum professionals' museum definitions and their aspirations towards museum visitors' motivations and outcomes.

Visitor Behaviour. Data extracts such as "museums used to stress me a lot" and "afraid to cross any lines" have been coded as *prejudice against actions in museums,* and that code has been mentioned 4 times. "Meet friends", "social reasons", "first date", and "having a small chat about the artworks" are some of the examples coded as *socialising in museum atmospheres,* and that code has been mentioned 16 times. The code *touristic activities or activities done during leisure time* has been mentioned 16 times and contains data extracts such as "weekends and school holidays", "free day out", "is on the bucket list for many people who come to visit" and "a great day out". Data extracts such as "I have definitely spoken to random people before", "yes, I have and sometimes catch them in the same group talking a bit longer with eachother *(sic)*" have been coded as *evidence of the possibility of making new friends in museums* and that code has been mentioned 11 times. The total amount of the codes used under the theme *visitor behaviour* is 47. The *visitor behaviour* theme describes museum professionals' observations in various circumstances on visitors, including time periods, motivations and if they may feel any type of prejudice and experiences on whether or not they have chances to socialise and make friends. Hence, making it possible to consider that given the possibility to socialise by the museum, bias may decrease, and a suitable environment may be created for making friends. According to Interviewee 09, "emotion of joy is a tabu in museums", while Interviewee 02 feels that they (museum visitors) must walk in a quiet and slow manner. Although these prejudices exist, museums are also considered to be social places as mentioned by Interviewee 04, meeting up with friends in museums is a social activity for families. Striking up a conversation together and comparing and sharing their experiences, spending some time together and meeting new people are some of the examples given for socialisation instances in museums. From the perspective of Interview 08 "ticking off the site from their 'must see' list" is a museum visitation reason much as making a day-long event for families is to Interviewee 02. Interviewee 04 states that they have clearly seen indications of people making friends in museums. "People could find like-minded friends, and we know that they (museum visitors) have often gone on to meet up outside the group". Interviewee 11 states that museums are places that can grant the opportunity of making friends. Including the aforementioned positive statements by the museum professionals concerning the possibility of making friends, it is highly probable to categorise museums as possible social environments if the opportunity is provided and bias is eliminated.

3   Conclusion

Social and gamified museums that offer immersive art experiences allow for identity exploration and social interactions through role-playing. The survey results point out that a vast majority of the participants' age group is between 18–34, more than half of the sample group visits museums rarely or sometimes, and the sample group plays games sometimes. The participants who do not visit museums have presented a lack of motivation, time, excitement, and stamina as some of the main reasons. Although the participants lack motivation, a conspicuous amount would like to make a new friend and play a game in a museum. Therefore, it is possible to state that introducing social and gamified opportunities may increase their motivation towards visiting museums.

The overwhelming majority of people surveyed have responded that they do not visit museums alone, similarly to previous studies, and that participants who visit with companions are more indulgent in making new friends and playing games in museums. Still, people who visit museums alone have reported that they have made friends more than other respondents. The data also indicates that elderly visitors prefer not to visit museums alone. As respondents look at artworks and read labels, they also interact with companions and use their mobile devices to take photos, check online sources or share content on social media platforms during museum visits.

Respondents have surveyed that some of their motivations to visit museums are touristic activities or day trips, education and learning, entertainment and enjoyment purposes. Similarly, museum professionals expect visitors to have a good and fruitful experience that would result in revisitation. Although museums offer various activities, events and workshops, the survey results show that these are not the primary motivations of museum visitors. Museums are places to see artworks/exhibitions, have fun and relax, according to the participants and are not defined as places to make new friends. However, the vast majority of the participants would like to make a new friend in a museum. Supporting these results, museum professionals have witnessed visitors willing to make new friends during museum events. There are noticeable differences between respondents who are open to making new friends and those who are unwilling. The participants who want to avoid making new friends are more prone to avoiding feelings of empathy, sympathy, creativity, and enjoyment, in addition to mainly visiting museums to retain information.

Research indicates that individuals who visit museums tend to enjoy engaging in interactive and entertaining activities, as well as socialising with other visitors and meeting new people while they explore the exhibits. Consequently, game-playing frequency does not significantly influence willingness to play games in museums. Museum professionals are also open to such activities as long as they are conducted within the limits of the rules and regulations. Both visitors and professionals desire positive emotions and seek to avoid negative emotions during their museum experience. Therefore, a friendly and inviting museum environment is of utmost importance in ensuring that visitors have an enjoyable and positive experience. A crucial aspect of achieving this could be the implementation of social and gamified features within the museum. By doing so, visitors are encouraged to engage with each other and the exhibits in a fun and interactive manner. Additionally, the provision of immersive art experiences adds a further layer of intrigue and excitement to the museum visit, further enhancing the overall visitor experience. Finally, museums should also strive to promote self-discovery and identity exploration amongst their visitors by providing opportunities for role-playing and interactive activities that encourage visitors to explore their identities and share their experiences with others.

References

1. Walker, K., Fróes, I.: The art of play: exploring the roles of technology and social play in museums. In: Museums at Play: Games, Interaction and Learning, Museums Etc, pp. 486–499 (2011)
2. Rounds, J.: Doing identity work in museums. Curator Museum J. **49**(2), 133–150 (2006). https://doi.org/10.1111/j.2151-6952.2006.tb00208.x
3. Museum Definition - International Council of Museums - International Council of Museums. https://icom.museum/en/resources/standards-guidelines/museum-definition/. Accessed 18 May 2023
4. Griffiths, J.-M., King, D.: InterConnections: the IMLS national study on the use of Libriaries, Museums and the Internet. Survey Methods Report (2008)
5. Bennett, J., Haron, S., Acdonald, M.: Behind the Scenes at the Science Museum. Materializing Culture, pp. xiii+293. Berg, Oxford and New York (2002). ISBN 1-85973-571-1. £14.00 (paperback).', The British Journal for the History of Science, vol. 37, no. 1, 2004, https://doi.org/10.1017/s0007087403215399
6. Pekarik, A.J., Doering, Z.D., Bickford, A.: 'Visitors' role in an exhibition debate: science in American life. Curator: Museum J. **42**(2), 117–129 (1999). https://doi.org/10.1111/j.2151-6952.1999.tb01135.x
7. Benjamin, W.: The Work of Art in the Age of Its Technological Reproducibility, and Other Writings on Media. The Belknap Press of Harvard University Press (2008)
8. Tuan, Y.-F.: Place: an experiential perspective. Geogr. Rev. **65**(2), 151–165 (1975). https://doi.org/10.2307/213970
9. Johnston, C.: What is social value?: a discussion paper/by Chris Johnston. In: Technical publications series (Australian Heritage Commission); no. 3. Canberra: A.G.P.S. (1992)
10. Huizinga, J.: Homo Ludens: A Study of the Play Element in Culture, 1st ed. Maurice Temple Smith Ltd., London (1949). https://doi.org/10.4324/9781315824161
11. Carlsson, R.: How the creative use of audio tours is attracting a new museum audience - MuseumNext (2020). https://www.museumnext.com/article/how-the-creative-use-of-audio-tours-is-attracting-a-new-museum-audience/. Accessed 10 May 2023
12. Gebbensleben, S., Dittmann, J., Vielhauer, C.: Multimodal audio guide for museums and exhibitions. Multimedia Mob. Devices II **6074**, 60740S (2006). https://doi.org/10.1117/12.641404
13. The Object Podcast — Minneapolis Institute of Art. https://new.artsmia.org/the-object-podcast/. Accessed 18 May 2023
14. Meet Me at the Museum | Podcast on Spotify. https://open.spotify.com/show/7xIg7hMY2oNUMVMBFAdzhD. Accessed 23 May 2023
15. How Spotify playlists became the new exhibition audio guides | The Art Newspaper. https://www.theartnewspaper.com/feature/the-new-audio-guide-a-spotify-playlist. Accessed 19 Mar 2023
16. Writing the Future | Museum of Fine Arts, Boston. https://www.mfa.org/exhibition/writing-the-future. Accessed 10 Mar 2023
17. Mortensen, M.F.: Designing immersion exhibits as border-crossing environments. Museum Manag. Curatorsh. **25**(3), 323–336 (2010). https://doi.org/10.1080/09647775.2010.498990
18. Belaën, F.: L'immersion au service des musées des sciences. In: Proceedings of the 7th International Cultural Heritage Informatics Meeting, pp. 1–17. Ecole du Louvre, Paris (2003)
19. Reflection. I am like you, I daresay. https://www.1944.pl/en/article/reflection.-i-am-like-you-i-daresay,5109.html. Accessed 17 May 2023
20. Bowman, S.L.: The Functions of Role-Playing Games: How Participants Create Community, Solve Problems and Explore Identity. Jefferson, N.C: McFarland & Co, USA (2010)

21. Scott, C.: Measuring social value. In: Sandell, R. (ed.) Museums, Society, Inequality. Abingdon, Oxon, UNITED STATES: Taylor & Francis Group (2002). http://ebookcentral.proquest.com/lib/tees/detail.action?docID=171037
22. Woodward, K., and I. C. T. Culture: Identity and Difference. Sage in Association with the Open University, London (1997)
23. Juul, J.: The magic circle and the puzzle piece (2008). https://publishup.uni-potsdam.de/frontdoor/index/index/docId/2554. 17 May 2023
24. Smith, L.F., Smith, J.K., Tinio, P.P.L.: Time spent viewing art and reading labels. Psychol Aesthet Creat Arts **11**(1) (2017). https://doi.org/10.1037/aca0000049
25. A guide to slow looking – In the Gallery|Tate. https://www.tate.org.uk/art/guide-slow-looking. Accessed 20 May 2023
26. Slow Art Day: Make Your Next Museum Visit More Mindful|Rubin Museum of Art (2016). https://rubinmuseum.org/blog/slow-art-day-make-your-next-museum-visit-more-mindful. Accessed 20 May 2023
27. Why Has Mobile Gaming Become So Popular With Players? https://gaminglyfe.com/why-has-mobile-gaming-become-so-popular-with-players/. Accessed 20 May 2023
28. Sofias smuggling. https://sofiassmuggling.de/. Accessed 20 May 2023
29. Akçalı, A., Iurgel, I.A., Sezen, T.: A Social App that Combines Dating and Museum Visiting Experiences, vol. 265. Springer, Cham (2019). https://doi.org/10.1007/978-3-030-06134-0_24
30. Braun, V., Clarke, V.: Using thematic analysis in psychology. Qual. Res. Psychol. **3**(2), 77–101 (2006). https://doi.org/10.1191/1478088706qp063oa

Future Content Delivery

'In the Future We Will Make Our Own Superheroes': Reflections on the Future of Broadcast for Children Aged 7–11

Dylan Yamada-Rice[1]([✉]) and Eleanor Dare[2]

[1] University of Plymouth, Plymouth, UK
dylan.yamada-rice@plymouth.ac.uk
[2] University of Cambridge, Cambridge, UK
erd46@cam.ac.uk

Abstract. Throughout 2022 and 2023, we worked with around 200 children to better understand the future of broadcast media for 7–11-year-olds in the UK. The work formed part of a wider Arts and Humanities Research Council (AHRC) funded project known as XR Stories and housed at the University of York. The project reported on here, resulted in several key findings related to (1) multi-materiality, (2) materiality and making work slows with Ai, (3) interaction and (4) mashed-up brands. This sits alongside our production of immersive applications, which emerged from deploying machine learning as a collaborative approach to broadcast media content production with children. These methods are highlighted in this article and we also show the reasons for valuing children's material engagement with epistemic processes connected to the senses. Indeed, this is an argument we make in relation to wider discussions in the field that the integration of artificial intelligence (AI) into many aspects of digital media production has led to numerous ethical dilemmas and concerns. The realm of children's media is no exception, as AI is increasingly used to generate initial broadcast media pitches, and increasingly the content. Children's ideas about the future are crucial in shaping our collective vision and actions. As theorists we draw upon Kress (2012, 1996); Barad, (2007); Nail (2020) and a range of practices and theories relating to worldbuilding and the ethical implications of AI technology. We also explore the ways in which worldbuilding and fictioning can be used to imagine and shape possible futures, and how emerging technologies might be integrated into these processes in a responsible, inclusive manner.

Keywords: Future Broadcast Media · Children's Media · AI · Design for Children · Arts-based Research

1 Introduction

In 2022–23 we were commissioned by the University of York's XR Stories to explore what children under 11-years-old want from future broadcast media. Our work in this area, sat alongside two other work packages, one called 'Untold Stories' led by Dr

D. Crawford et al. (Eds.): TIE 2023, LNICST 575, pp. 127–145, 2024.
https://doi.org/10.1007/978-3-031-59383-3_9

Becky Parry with Chol Theatre and Arts Company that invited groups of young women to imagine the future of broadcasting as a means of storytelling. The other, named 'Interactive Broadcast Futures', was led by Dr Rob Eagle and the British Film Institute, and sought to understand how Gen Z audiences envisioned future formats and technologies of screen-based entertainment using a hackathon format.

Our project was framed within the context of a decline in children watching linear TV and the planned closing of linear broadcasting of CBBC in 2025/6. Also, within the rise of broadcast media and other industries connected to filmmaking, theatre and gaming to seek new ways of reaching audiences with emerging technologies.

Our insight into children's ideas in this area was achieved by running a series of public engagement workshops for groups of children at the National Science and Media Museum in Bradford. Here, we offered children the opportunity to explore their ideas on the future of broadcast media in relation to a series of new technologies such as Photogrammetry, Augmented Reality (AR), Cardboard VR (age appropriate) and a proto-metaverse, online gaming platform called Roblox. Within this context participants were given the opportunity to explore these technologies through a series of hands-on art and design-based research methods.

The intention of these workshops was to seek an understanding of children's ideas for how they would like to consume future broadcast media for entertainment, using a two-prong focus on (1) engagement via immersion (i.e., VR) and (2) via interaction (i.e. mass online gaming platforms). This article is structured firstly to outline the methodology, ethics and means of analysis, and then the four key findings that emerged from the data.

2   Methodology, Ethics and Analysis

This section describes the context, methods, ethical considerations and means of analysis applied to the data.

2.1   Context: Heritage Brands and Future Broadcasting Possibilities

Our investigation of this topic focused on using the Beano as a case study. This is because the Beano can be classed as a heritage brand. Brand heritage is a concept within the marketing discipline, which suggests that the consumer appeal of products and services offered by older companies may be enhanced by the historical characters of their brands (Hudson, 2011; Urde et al., 2007 in Hudson, 2015) [1, 2].

In the case of the Beano, which was launched in 1938, this would suggest enhanced interest in maintaining the historical brand. Additionally, it is a good illustration of a brand that has already withstood reincarnations, such as from comics to TV shows and apps. Thus, this history provided the context for exploration of how emerging technologies might shift and change the brand again. However, using the brand as the basis for the workshop also had limitations in that it was not most children under 11years-old favourite content, and although nearly all parents/grandparent we spoke to knew of the brand not all the child-participants did. In retrospect using children's favourite brands, even if not heritage might have yielded additional findings.

2.2 Aims and Objectives

The overall aims of the project were to:

undertake public engagement activities on the topic of future media broadcast.

explore how children under 11-years-old would like to consume heritage brands through interactive media and, or new technologies.

To achieve these aims the following research questions were asked:

1 What are the elements most important to children under 11-years-old when changing heritage brands into interactive media?
2 What are the elements most important to children under 11-years-old when changing heritage brands to immersive media?

2.3 Methods

In relation to seeking children's ideas on what comes next and what they imagined the future of traditional forms of media content, such as TV to look like, we created a research methodology based around a series of public engagement workshops where children and families could opt in when visiting the National Science and Media Museum in Bradford. Here, we asked children to think about what emerging technologies might mean for the future of broadcast content aimed at them, through a series of cultural probes (Wyeth & Diercke, 2006; Gaver et al. 1999; Gaver et al., 2004), [3–5] that is a collection of visual

Fig. 1. Cultural Probes used in the public engagement workshops

and physical materials that act as a prompt to engage non-design specialist participants in design processes. Examples of these are shown in Fig. 1:

Simultaneously, this was framed as a method of co-design building on two principles that can be helpful for including children in speculative research as outlined by Van Mechelen (2016) [6]:

As a method or technique, co-design relies on two major assumptions. Firstly, that everyone can be creative, but many are not in the habit of using or expressing their creativity, and secondly, making creativity more open and social through participatory processes increase positive outcomes (e.g. the range and quality) (p. 6).

These were applied to all four workshops that crossed two themes, (1) character creation and (2) worldbuilding. These are outlined next.

2.3.1 Public Engagement Workshops: Character Creation

The first two workshops (see Fig. 2) focused on changing Beano characters into future broadcasting prototypes using photogrammetry. Children who attended the public engagement workshops were given a range of cultural probes that consisted of a range of stories and characters from the Beano and asked to create models using Play-Doh or LEGO, of those they would like to form part of interactive and immersive digital or virtual worlds. In doing so, we also drew on ideas from speculative design (Dunne and Raby, 2013; Wargo and Alvarado, 2020) [7, 8] where children were asked to use designing and making to explore the unknown future of broadcast media.

Fig. 2. Public engagement workshop set-up

In terms of introducing children to emerging technologies, children's character designs were scanned using a photogrammetry app (and also photographed as a data collection record) and we showed children how this turned their creations using familiar analogue materials into 3D digital assets that could be used within virtual reality and or gaming spaces (Fig. 3).

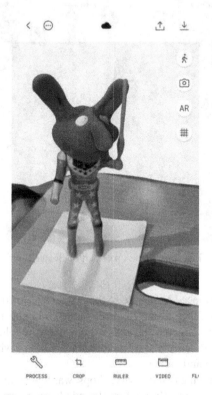

Fig. 3. Example of a photogrammetry scan

Introducing participants to photogrammetry was also seen as offering insight into emerging tools for storytelling that could form part of future broadcast media.

2.3.2 Public Engagement Workshops: Worldbuilding

The third and fourth workshops focused on the creation of buildings and objects for a future Beano Town. Using the same cultural probes as were used during the first two workshops (see Fig. 1), participants were asked to create buildings they wished to remain in the future broadcasting of the Beano by using cardboard boxes or they could also create entirely new ideas. There was also the option of creating objects needed in the town from Play-Doh.

Once completed, participants added their building to those made by other children to collectively create Future Beano Town (Fig. 4).

Fig. 4. A close-up of part of Beano Town

The buildings were placed in a circle so they could be filmed in 360 and then viewed in Virtual Reality (VR) if they wanted to. From here, children's models were once again scanned using a photogrammetry app and participants were told how the assets created would form part of a VR space and a Roblox game. Both of which proved to motivate children further to build and create.

Our intention, as with the first two workshops, was that by including techniques such as world-building, 360-degree filming for VR and photogrammetry, we are introducing children in Bradford to a range of techniques commonly used by adults in the design and production of new forms of storytelling media. Thus, demonstrating that their ideas are valued but also demystifying new technologies and for many bringing them into contact with them for the first time.

As Hickey-Moody et al. (2021) [9] reminds us 'interpreting children's artwork isn't easy, and attempting to make sense of seemingly disparate or unrelated elements can be daunting. Alternative and even contradictory interpretations are often possible' (p. 1387). But children's artefacts, observations, making processes and agency as artists make them 'valued sources and producers of knowledge, including experiential, material, embodied and affective knowledge, as well as more traditional forms of cultural, political, discursive and ideological knowledge' (ibid, 2021). Our approach to children's knowledge and engagement with materials might be defined as a 'facet method-ology' (Mason, 2011) [10], in which the metaphor of a faceted gemstone is used to 'characterise an approach to methods and analysis that offers insight into the multi-dimensionality of everyday life.

The gemstone is conceived of as the overall research question, with the different planes of the gemstone being different approaches to look at the same question' (Woodward, 2020, p. 146) [11].

Thus, our facet methodology deployed character creation, worldbuilding, digital interaction, drawing, playing, observation, conversation, cultural probes, questions, curation, intergenerational making and visual/material analysis. As Woodward (2020) [12] writes, such an approach:

> ...does not aim to produce comprehensive descriptive accounts of a topic, but rather to produce flashes of insight, which may arise through taking unconventional approaches to a topic, or through a combination of approaches. The insights may be unexpected but arise through the creativity of the researcher in thinking about methods of analysis and approaching the research question (p. 146).

The insights gained from our facet methodology also informed the development of research - responsive media -VR and AR experiences, animations, 3D models, ai generated extensions to children's designs and Roblox worlds, which are described next.

2.3.3 Developing Future Broadcast Media Prototypes

The outputs from the combined workshops gave us characters and story world assets, which we went on to explore in relation to creating immersive and interactive spaces using emerging technologies, and to consider the role of both interaction and immersion, separately and combined.

For example, Dare hand-animated children's models so that they formed part of an augmented reality experience as well as two VR experiences, one with Oculus Quest and one designed for the inexpensive and thus readily accessible Google Cardboard systems, which work with mobile phones (Fig. 5).

Fig. 5. VR Beano Town created with children's models (Dare)

Whereas Yamada-Rice used them to create an interactive game within Roblox (Fig. 6), a so-called prototype metaverse for its seemingly endless possibilities for playing and socialising online.

Fig. 6. Roblox Beano Town created with children's models (Yamada-Rice)

These were seen by us as experiments in thinking about how children's creations and ideas could be included directly into the future of broadcast media. Finally, children were given the opportunity to try out these spaces so that we could gain further insight into their thoughts.

2.4 Innovation and Ethical Consideration

Across the course of the workshops, we estimate that we worked with at least 200 children and families. Our approach was to allow anyone attending the museum on the day that the workshops were being held to drop in or out at will. This meant that some children stayed for a long period of time while others came and watched while an older or younger sibling joined in. The nature of self-selecting for the workshops also meant participants were able to invest as much or as little time as they wanted, and this was seen as being inclusive of individual needs and at the heart of good ethical practices.

Methodological originality and advancement draw upon our commitment to developing engaging ways of including children in research and co-design processes. It also responds to the UN Rights of the Child (1989) [13] that stipulates children should be included in areas that directly affect them. In relation to this, we advocate for the exploration of new research and design methods that better match the natural communication and play patterns of children rather than using simplified versions of methods that were originally designed for adults (Yamada-Rice, 2021) [14]. Previously we extended the research method of cultural probes (Gaver, 1999) [4] by linking it to story-worlding methods to effectively include children in narrative development. This time we went further to explore how combining the concepts of cultural probes as a method with knowledge about how emerging technologies are being experimented within immersive storytelling practices (where both our work is situated) created an interactive means of data collection and co-design of possibilities for future ways of broadcasting (in this case the Beano) with children and their families.

By bringing playful ways of making such as through the use of Play-Doh, LEGO and cardboard and merging these with new forms of storytelling and representation afforded by AR, VR and online gaming platforms we afforded children the opportunity to be involved at every stage of production as researchers of these new forms of representation. These ideas are supported by Aarseth (1997) [15] who is rigorous in his critique of previous theoretical arguments that have created false dichotomies between analogue and digital texts, this is a useful frame of reference for this project, and Aarseth's taxonomy has potential as a framework for our own work with new forms of storytelling. The dynamic stability/instability of co-created texts mediated by Augmented and Virtual Reality provides scope for us to generate original and much needed new analysis of emerging technology and children's experience of immersion that are needed by re-searchers and industry but in this project fed directly into our planned experimental development.

2.5 Approaches to Data Analysis

Data collection was messy due to the large number of children that took part and also because some chose to do one part of an activity while others did everything. In general, data consisted of children's models made from physical materials, 3D assets of most models (but not all; some took their models home before we had time to scan them) and field notes of conversations had with children and families. The models were analysed using Visual Content Analysis which seeks to quantify 'relative frequency of visual representation using variables and values defined by the researcher(s)' (Bell, 2001, p. 10) [16].

Specifically, children's character designs produced as part of the first two public engagement workshops were analysed using the variables defined as (1) theme, i.e., was it a Beano character, an original character designed by the child, a character from a different brand or a non-character (e.g., a volcano), (2) materials used, i.e., Play-Doh, drawing or mixed media. No values were applied to the data since we did not collect information about the participants who had made them. A total of 37 models formed this dataset.

With respect to children's world building models these were analysed using variables defined as (1) theme, i.e. type of building and (2) material used, i.e. Play-Doh or mixed media. Again, no values were applied. A total of 49 models formed this dataset.

Additonally, field notes and small clips of audio sound design were rudimentarily analysed using Braun and Clark's (2006) [17] thematic analysis, Then, once all the datasets were compared to one another the emerging themes were identified as:

1. Multi-materiality and immersion
2. Interaction
3. Mashed-up brands

We then added an additional theme that emerged from analysing our own involvement in the research process of using children's outputs in online game content, virtual and augmented reality and experimenting with AI, which appears also to have a connection to ideas of the future of broadcast media. This is:

3   Materiality and Making Workflows with AI

These emerging themes should be seen in the context that we believe children's material culture is more than its reduction to language, 'material culture is durable and physical; textual ways of approaching objects cannot access these material endurances and re-sistances; things resist symbolism or even use value as objects can be ambiguous' (Woodward, 2020, p. 150) [11].

This was evident in our analysis of children's responses to Beano comics (in the cultural probes), which they used as both orthodox texts, to read and look at, but also as materials transformed into windows, TV screens, house facades and as a surface upon which they drew, or a scaffold structure to hold together assemblages of Play-Doh, found materials, small toys and drawings.

This points to the multimedia and multimodal nature of children's experience of storytelling and mediation, which can be described as an assemblage, also incorporating other humans, objects, technical and social systems and culture. Bennett (2010) [18] writes:

Assemblages are not governed by any central head: no one materiality or type of mate-rial has sufficient competence to determine consistently the trajectory or impact of the group. The effects generated by an assemblage are, rather, emergent properties, emergent in that their ability to make something happen.

(Bennett, 2010, p. 24) [19].

Such contingency and fluidity were evident in the way children and adults worked together to create their complex worlds at the National Museum of Science and Media, often drawing in and around and over each other's work, with and without spoken interaction, sometimes referring to the Beano comics in the workshop or things they had seen in the museum or in other places, such as games and shops. Our data analysis reflects the bricolage of materials, individuals, environments and media cultures which were manifest in these workshops. For example, Dare experimented with using workshop models with AI software to explore how children, designers of children's future broadcast media and machine learning might be integrated in the future. In this way emerging softwares such as Run-wayML can be seen to combine with technologies, children, and us as artists and re-searchers as a further extension to the assemblages.

4   Research Findings

This section describes in more detail some initial thoughts in relation to key findings to emerge from the public engagement workshops. These are (1) multi-materiality and immersion, (2) materiality and making workflows with AI, (3) interaction and (4) mashed-up brands.

4.1 Multi-materiality and Immersion

Kress (2010) [20] states us that all communication is based on historic cultural and social practices. This is a solid reminder that when we look at what is happening in the present or want to predict the future of communication (including storytelling) then we must embed this alongside knowledge of the past. Relatedly, the opening chapter of "Shivers down your spine: cinema, museums and the immersive view":

> ..compares the spectacular of cathedrals to important themes for immersivity 'including spectatorship, immersion, the reenactment, virtual travel visual excess, mimesis, the uncanny, and death...in light of these factors, it would be remiss of me not to consider the cathedral as a hugely significant pre-cinematic site of immersive viewing experiences
>
> (Griffiths, 2008, n.p) [21].

Griffiths (2008) [12] continues by describing how the sense of immersion brought about in cathedrals is a multi-artisan feat in which stained glass window makers, architects, builders, sculptors, calligraphers and painters come together to pull it off. The same is true of artists, technologists, developers, designers and writers working together today to think about what emerging technologies might mean for the future of broadcast me-dia. In our own work experimenting in this field, we played around with the affordances of new and old technologies and materials, and tried to understand what happens when they are combined in various ways. Child-participants in this project did the same. As described in this paper, children used any of the materials offered to them, both analogue, digital and virtual to respond to our request to imagine what the Beano might look like in the future, for example, when a child has combined two different toys with Play-Doh to create their character design of future Minnie the Minx (Fig. 7).

Fig. 7. Future Minnie the Minx

Similar examples existed when children created their own original characters too, where combining existing toys with Play-Doh used the best affordances of each to make something entirely new. Out of the 49 buildings made by participants, 21 were mixed media. Combining materials in this way was different than we had anticipated when designing the workshops and thought cardboard would be used for making buildings and Play-Doh for objects such as trees etc. in the Beano Town scene. This is an example of how children's ideas often differ from adult's and is a reminder of why we must keep them involved in research that affects them.

As materials got more scarce children began using anything that was to hand, including tearing up the comics we had included in the cultural probes and the Play-Doh pot lids. These multiple materials were combined with making, whilst engaged in stories about the Beano and their own original storytelling as they made. In some ways this reflects the literature of live cinema that suggests its popularity over traditional cinema is in the opportunities for the audience to interact with each other not only the screen story. Additionally, the opportunity to take the Beano stories and engage with them through physical materials appeared to immerse the children in the subject of the workshops on what they want from the future of media broadcast, as well as in the context for this exploration, which was the Beano stories. This was similar to a finding from an earlier project undertaken by Yamada-Rice et al. (2019) [22] that looked at the role of makerspaces for children to understand and create with virtual reality and found that for children the opportunity to create with analogue materials and an open brief was as immersive as the "immersive" technologies at the centre of the work.

It is worth noting that families, including parents, siblings, grandparents and family friends were all active participants working with the child-participants. When asked if they knew of the Beano, it was clear that this was a familiar heritage brand, and we speculate that this was part of the reason families were drawn into making together. As a result, we hypothesise that future media broadcasting could do well to consider how heritage brands might play a role in creating opportunities for shared cross-generational experiences. Similarly, including physical materials as part of exploration of emerging technologies also aided cross-generational exploration of the topic as they are accessible to anyone.

We made a deliberate choice to include physical materials, alongside our exploration of the role of emerging technologies in future broadcast media. The reason for this was two-fold. On the one hand it was a practical decision in as far as we would not have access to enough technologies or staff to aid everyone to work with digital technologies at the same time. The second reason was for accessibility, we were aware that our workshops were taking place in Bradford, and that it has been reported that in Yorkshire 'tens of thousands of families are without a laptop or device' (Parsons, 2021, n.p) [23], meaning using emerging technologies is likely to have been new for many and thus physical materials could act as a way of scaffolding their use.

The findings showed that children were fully interested in trying out emerging technologies. In particular child-participants were excited to see other children's models in both the virtual space created by Dare and the Roblox space created by Yamada-Rice.

The photogrammetry app we used as part of our methodology was simple enough for children to create immediate outputs with physical materials to be used in digital spaces. Placing children's physical models into these digital spaces made with Unity and Roblox Studio creates a jarring awkward aesthetic compared to the usual digital aesthetics they foreground (see Fig. 6). However, child-participants talked with great excitement when they came across their models for the first time.

"Wow I can see the Play-Doh people"

"I just made a post office [out of cardboard] let me see if I can find it [in the Roblox game]".

(Child-participants)

Such findings are a good reminder that we must not take the current mechanics or aesthetics being developed by adults in the tech industry as set in stone. This supports arguments in our previous work where we reported:

...on two new frameworks for developing Immersive Visual Story (IVS) worlds. These frameworks are designed to challenge the development and theorising of IVS spaces... Building on the work of Alston (2016) [24] and Keogh & Nicolls (2019) [25] we provide alternative structures for IVS development frameworks that are led by Game Engines such as Unity, Unreal and Roblox that arguably construct a particular set of subjectivities through their templates and menus, their models of subjects, their business models, spatialities, workflows, audio systems, rendering engines and modes of interaction, which Keogh and Nicoll (2019) [25] describe as 'Circuits of cultural software.

(Dare & Yamada-Rice, 2023, n.p) [26]

Only three children we asked had not used Roblox, showing the huge presence online game worlds have in children's lives. However, despite the opportunity to use Roblox, try virtual or augmented reality or use photogrammetry, children's love of creating with cardboard and Play-Doh was no less depleted than it has ever been. Perhaps because opportunities to make with physical materials have been marginalised in favour of STEM and STEAM subjects in education, children showed real excitement at creating with physical materials.

This finding led us to further consider that whereas formal education, including higher education (where we both teach) are making an artificial divide between analogue and digital making, which was not the case for children who seamlessly enjoyed blending the two. Indeed, it is not the case for many creative professionals either. As AI begins to emerge and impact on the ways in which we create and consume content it is also worth noting that the best examples of AI use are when artists collaborate with it (Main et al., 2022), much in the way we invited children to create through our methodology. The next section describes more about materiality and making with AI, which will arguably impact greatly on the workflows involved in future media production.

4.2 Materiality and Making Workflows with AI

Observing and working with children to create models and build speculative worlds and processes is to become acutely aware that the idea of humans and non-humans existing as discrete entities is 'based upon a worldview grounded in hierarchical subject–object relationships' (Myers, 2019, p. 21) [27]. To question the hierarchy of humans and non-human relations is arguably to shift away from an adult ontology to one in which the boundaries between materials and humans, non-human animals, objects and locations becomes much more fluid, one in which our understanding of technologies, stories and mediation can be creatively expanded upon.

In turn, this disruption of hierarchies might also shift our conception of agency, production, audienceship, authorship and directorship for the future of broadcast. But this does not mean it should occlude the asymmetrical nature of power relations entangled with technologies and their political and economic contexts and drivers, especially in relation to children.

In line with a new materialist turn (Coole & Frost, 2010) [28] which incorporates and entangles the social and the material (Barad, 2007) [29], it is fruitful to ask how the future of broadcast for children might unfold if it acknowledges and works with a new materialist ontology.

Throughout the research project we experimented with new and emerging digital-analogue workflows, including machine learnt processes of animation via interpolation in RunwayML (a machine learning platform for artists and designers), text-to-3D model algorithms, such as Mirage, Deforum and Stable Dream Fusion (Poole et al., 2022) [30], MonsterMesh, a Beta sketch based tool for drawing and animating 3D meshes online, which has enabled an effective transit from analogue to digital 3D models for VR and AR.

Stable Diffusion (a machine learning image synthesis application) in Unity and Blender has further supported an efficient and materially different process of asset development, one which has the potential to make games and digital storytelling much more accessible to children and adults. But there are also very serious ethical issues entangled with machine learning, as discussed at the end of this section.

Myers (2019) [27] describes a form of knowledge in children's making which is 'continually enmeshed with the various apparatuses of inquiry' which was 'not about uncovering what pre-existed our investigations, but about producing something different in our intra-activity-tracing, adding, making a different frame. What can be known is bound up in the material-discursive processes of inquiry' (Myers, 2019, p. 275) [27]. Combining analogue and digital processes and materials we draw upon expanded ideas of causality and interaction 'which are also relevant to digital works and to a reconsideration of interactivity in terms of its meanings, its goals and some of the orthodoxies that have established themselves in relation to notions of the interactive' (Dare, 2020, n.p.) [31].

Karen Barad's Agential Realism and a notion of 'performative' understanding changes our conception of how mediation unfolds, shifting to a form of meaning-making rooted in events, practices and real-world actions which 'branches away from forms of representation that place us outside of the world: it places us firmly as part of the 'world in which we have our being' (Barad, 2007, p. 133) [29]. According to Barad, intra-action, unlike interaction, does not presuppose 'the prior existence of independent entities of relata' (ibid, p. 139) [12]. Barad does not take for granted atomistic or Cartesian separations between subject and object, but, instead, sees situations and actions as allowing phenomenological relata to emerge as specific causal intra-actions (Dare, 2020) [31].

Children's apparently innate capacity for play suggests a different relationship to mediation and materials which is potentially less (stereotypically) passive than adults, in which objects and toys, things and 'materials – as they come into being and are transformed through relations with other things and people – are an inextricable aspect of who we are, our social relations, and even our humanity' (Woodward, 2020, p. 1) [11]. Thus, there are possibilities for children's ideas to be directly used and then altered by AI to be included directly within future media production.

Yet, deploying AI in children's media raises many ethical issues, relating to the extraction of natural resources required to power huge datasets, the exploitation of 'Ghost' (Gray et al., 2019) [32] workers and the underlying logic of Machine Learning which currently replicates colonial categorisations, often racialised with a lineage going back to slavery (Benjamin, 2019) [33]. But there are also issues of copyright and representation, with machine learning models often replicating stereotypes and patterns of exclusion. Using new media workflows ethically, with and for children, necessitates an understanding of technical procedures but also a non-trivial grasp of their complex social and economic contexts. Future broadcast media will require nuanced reframing of concepts such as digital and media literacy and an understanding of data and media infrastructures.

Woodward's questions and research strategies have been useful for us, to 'engage with the capacities of things and materials to develop provocative methods of generating data' (Woodward, 2020, p. 11) [11]. For Woodward, as arguably for all researchers, when 'things are understood in this way they are always becoming within changing environments; in this framework what people do with things – practices – are part of the things themselves. The definition of things as changing and emergent is in part a reaction against the taken-for-grantedness of things – their presumed solidity' (p. 14) [11]. Applied to a kinetic conception of media as conceived by Nail (2019) [34], fluidity and constant change are key features of kinetic media, distinguishing it from traditional static images or stable subjects.

The kinetic image (and all kinetic media) allows us to see the embodied subject in new and dynamic ways and has the potential to challenge traditional understandings of the body/audience/maker as a stable, fixed entity, but it also changes our ontology of images and wider media. With embedded text to image, which we foresee as emerging features of game engines and software such as Blender and Photoshop, media become explicitly multi-stable, conducive to multiple states within the same system, this is not to assert a radical discontinuity from previous systems, but to recognise an emerging pattern of media development which is likely to impact many different aspects of children's media production and reception.

4.3   Interaction

Thoughts on interaction were present from the start of the project when exploring ideas on why linear TV is in decline for children and what it is being replaced by. At the time of the study Yamada-Rice was working part-time for a research and digital content creation company specialising in the kid's market. Over the last couple of years, she witnessed changes brought into the space by massive online gaming platforms, but especially

Roblox, data from Influencer Marketing Hub shows that the platform had 45.5 million daily users recorded in 2022 with larger projections predicted for this year.

What is different about traditional TV viewing and contemporary gaming trends is that online games allow distanced social interactions to take place whilst engaging with content. Further, this not only relates to content for entertainment but also advertising, where brands seek to make experiences in-game that serve to drive consumption off-line.

We propose expanded ideas of causality and interaction and a reconsideration of the ways in which interactivity can be deployed and defined, for example, counterbalancing the notion of individual audience/producer choice with more collective processes and less overt or conventionally individualised forms of 'user' control. Espen Aarseth also challenges the term 'interactive', analysing the complex nature of boundaries between users, consumers and producers; 'to elevate a consumer group to producerhood' writes Aarseth (1997) [15]:

> …is a bold political statement; and in the production and consumption of symbolic artefacts (texts) the boundary between these positions becomes a highly contested ground.
>
> (Aarseth, 1997, p. 163) [15]

Aarseth warns us of the danger inherent in applying terms from traditional literary theory to new forms of storytelling, and suggests that our understanding of 'agency' requires rethinking. We see direct connections to new and emerging forms of mediation, and like Aarseth (1997) [12], are wary of technological determinism and hyperbolic idealisation of co-production.

However, we do think the question of agency, effort and skill is significant, echoing some aspects of Aarseth's term ergodic, developed in response to emerging forms of interactive narrative, 25 years ago. In 1997, Aarseth defined ergodic texts as those in which the reader must work nontrivially to find a path through them (the word Ergodic comes from the Greek words for work and path). Today, we ask to what extent audiences wish to become producers or 'prosumers' of content and experiences, to what extent are children, in particular 7–11-years-olds, engaged by such modalities, and is the idea of children as active producers of broadcast content a form of exploitation or inculcation to neoliberalized ideas of near unceasing, networked labour?

The Covid-19 Pandemic, it seems, has swiftly changed our relationship to networked modalities of communication, to online platforms and interactions, for example, the UK government backlash against working remotely (Neate, 2022) [35], surfaces an ambivalence towards technology and modes of working/studying from afar that were once held up as future facing. Thus, interaction is both a driving force for new and emerging media consumption but also requires deep ethical consideration, particularly with regards to content made with or for children.

4.4 Mashed-up Brands

The final point to make is that some children sought to create the most playful and engaging experiences regardless of brand. So, whilst we were working with the Beano as a focus for the workshops, this did not limit children to thinking their ideas had to be confined to this brand. In the examples below, one child chose to make Mario House and another a home for Sponge Bob (Fig. 8) for Beano Town.

Fig. 8. Sponge Bob House

When asked about the decisions around this, children talked about their love of brands combining for limited edition content etc. Again, this relates to ideas from Kress in his earlier writing (1996) [36] where he talks about children using whatever is around them to make, play and communicate, a complete "mash-up", regardless of the original intention for their use made by adults. It also raises questions around copyright and how this will be adapted for future broadcast media.

5   Conclusions

The findings seem to suggest that as with other work that has gone before (e.g., Alston, 2016; Keogh & Nicolls, 2019; Dare & Yamada-Rice, 2023) [24–26], we must not take the design of immersive story worlds used for broadcast media as set in stone and instead seek alternatives to ensure they match all audience's needs. Sicart (2022) [37] states:

'Anything that is part of the practice of play gets its meaning and its ontology from that concrete technosocial situated arrangement of human agency, artificial agency, and materials'. This project has addressed the entanglement of materials and children in the production and reception of stories as a form of play, mediated in a dynamic flow between and within analogue, digital, virtual contexts, materials and pro-cesses. In such a configuration, 'new objects come into being as a consequence of a playful relational material entanglement' (ibid) [37].

In our work with children, we have observed such entanglement in the material practice of play and making, storytelling and remediation. We have observed the ways in which children deploy materials without caring for rigid ideas about their intended use, such as the lids and packaging of Play-Doh pots or using collaged Beano comics to create windows and parts of buildings in their models. These observations and our own experiences of making, playing and working with media, materials and emergent technologies offer a forward-facing framework for the Future of Broadcast for 7–11-year-olds, but we also acknowledge and value analogue traditions of storytelling and have seen how children and their parents/carers enjoy intergenerational experiences of films and television programmes, as well as making models and stories together.

We have identified an intensifying use of Machine Learning models for the production of media, and indeed, are in the midst of an intense hype cycle as we write, with Open AI releasing successive versions of their Large Language Model, Chat GPT, throughout the development of this research.

These models, while we have the resources to run them, are changing the workflows as well as the aesthetic, legal, processual and durational nature of media production; They may open up creation to some children, while gatekeeping it away from others, as we predict the almost inevitable appearance of pay walls which will proceed free Beta versions. With these technologies comes the need for interpersonal, infrastructural and structural literacies and ethics. Children will mature to find themselves navigating changed workplaces as well as changed workflows, with a tendency towards precarious labour entangled with automation (Suri & Gray, 2020) [32].

We see the need for children to be included in decisions about the future and present of media/broadcast, including the kind of content and interaction models, themes and modalities of transmission, representation and ethics, and the environmental impact, of for example, Big Data, server farms, blockchains and Metaverse technologies. Children have a right, we assert, to understand the planetary impact of these technologies as well as their potential for the future of broadcast.

References

1. Hudson, B.T.: Brand heritage. In: Cooper, C.L. (ed.) Wiley Encyclopaedia of Management (2015)
2. Urde, M., Greyser, S.A., Balmer, J.M.T.: Corporate brands with a heritage. J. Brand Manag. **15**(1), 4–19 (2007)
3. Wyeth, P. Diercke, C.: Designing cultural probes for children. In: OZCHI 2006 Proceedings ISBN: 1–59593–545–2 (2006)
4. Gaver, W., Dunne, T., Pacenti, E.: Cultural probes. Interactions **6**(1), 21–29 (1999)
5. Gaver, W., Boucher, A., Pennington, S., Walker, B.: Cultural probes and the value of uncertainty. Interactions **11**(5), 53–56 (2004)
6. Van Mechelen, M.: Designing technologies for and with children: a toolkit to prepare and conduct co-design activities and analyse the outcomes. Published online by Mintlab (2016)
7. Dunne, A., Raby, F.: Speculative Everything: Design, Fiction and Social Dreaming. MIT Press, Cambridge (2013)
8. Wargo, J.M., Alvarado, J.: Making as worlding: young children composing change through speculative design. Literacy **54**, 13–21 (2020)
9. Hickey-Moody, A., Horn, C., Willcox, M., Florence, E.: Arts-Based Methods for Research with Children (Studies in Childhood and Youth) Springer International Pub-lishing. Kindle Edition (2021)

10. Mason, J.: Facet methodology: the case for an inventive research orientation. Methodol. Innovat. Online **3**, 75–92 (2011)
11. Woodward, S.: Material Methods. SAGE Publications, New Delhi (2020)
12. Ibid
13. UN Rights of the Child (1989)
14. Yamada-Rice, D.: Children's interactive storytelling in Virtual Reality. Multimodality Soc. **1**(1), 48–67 (2021)
15. Aarseth, E.J.: Cybertext: Perspectives on Ergodic Literature. John Hopkins University Press, Baltimore (1997)
16. Bell, P.: Content analysis of visual images. In: van Leeiwen, T., Jewitt, C. (eds.) Handbook of Visual Analysis. SAGE, London (2001)
17. Braun, V., Clarke, V.: Using thematic analysis in psychology. Qualit. Res. Psychol. **3**(2), 77–101 (2006)
18. Bennett, J.: Vibrant Matter (a John Hope Franklin Center Book). Duke University Press, Durham (2010)
19. Ibid, p. 24
20. Kress, G.: Multimodality: A Social Semiotic Approach to Contemporary Communication. Routledge, London (2010)
21. Griffiths, A.: Shivers Down Your Spine: Cinema, Museums, and the Immersive View. Columbia University Press, New York (2008)
22. Yamada-Rice, D., Rodrigues, D., Zubrycka, J.: Makerspaces and virtual reality, Chapter 5. In: Blum-Ross, A., Kumpulainen, K., Marsh, J. (eds.) Enhancing digital Literacy and Creativity: Makerspaces in the Early Years. Routledge (2019)
23. Parsons, R.: Why the pandemic has exposed the scale of Yorkshire's digital divide. Yorkshire Post (2021). https://www.yorkshirepost.co.uk/education/why-the-pandemic-has-exposed-the-scale-of-yorkshires-digital-divide-3091347. Accessed 19 Mar 2023
24. Alston, A.: Beyond Immersive Theatre, Aesthetics, Politics and Productive Participation. Macmillan UK. Kindle Edition, London (2016)
25. Keogh, B., Nicoll, B.: The Unity Game Engine and the Circuits of Cultural Software. Palgrave Macmillan. Kindle Edition, Cham (2019)
26. Dare, E., Yamada-Rice, D.: Queer Psycho and the HE Circus: Applying Queering, Magic and More-than-Human Theories to Immersive Visual Story Worlds as an Anti-dote to Late Capitalism. Presence, MIT. (2023)
27. Myers, C.: Children and Materialities: The Force of the More-than-human in Children's Classroom Lives (Children: Global Posthumanist Perspectives and Materialist Theories). Springer, Singapore (2019). https://doi.org/10.1007/978-981-13-8168-3
28. Coole, D. H., & Frost, S. New materialisms: Ontology, Agency, and Politics. Durham: Duke University Press, London (2010)
29. Barad, K.: Meeting the Universe Halfway. Duke University Press, Durham (2007)
30. Poole, B., Jain, A., Barron, J.T., Mildenhall, B.: Text-to-3D using 2D Diffusion. arXiv:2209.14988 (2022)
31. Dare, E.: Diffracting virtual realities. Perform. Res. **25**(5), 101 (2020)
32. Suri, S., Gray, M.L.: Ghost Work: How to Stop Silicon Valley from Building a New Global Underclass. Harper Business, New York (2019)
33. Benjamin, R.: Race After Technology: Abolitionist Tools for the New Jim Code. Polity Press, Cambridge (2019)
34. Nail, T.: Theory of the Image. Oxford University Press, Oxford (2019)
35. Neate, R.: Out of office? How working from home has divided Britain. The Guardian (2022)
36. Kress, G.: Before writing. Rethinking the Paths to Literacy. Routledge, London (1996)
37. Sicart, M.: Playthings. Games Cult. **17**(1), 140–155 (2022)

Flexilink: A Low Latency Solution for Packet Based Media

John Grant[1]([⊠]) and Jeremy Foss[2]

[1] Nine Tiles, Cambridge, UK
j@ninetiles.com
[2] Birmingham City University, Birmingham, UK
jeremy.foss2@bcu.ac.uk

Abstract. Precise live audio collaboration over networks for professional applications has become practically (and theoretically) impossible with the widespread adoption of IP-based packet technologies. Traditional approaches used solutions based on the layer 2 (link layer). These protocols included AES50 [1] and MADI, and use a time-slot-based approach (similar to Time Division Multiplexing). However, the IP-based "best-effort" approach is subject to quality of service (QoS) availabilities in the network since data packets are required to queue in buffers in switching nodes as they progress through the network. This builds up an unpredictable degree of end-to-end latency for audio data through the network.

This paper sets out a unified low latency network architecture that simultaneously supports both time deterministic media data and also the remaining best effort traffic; both traffic types can co-exist and be transported in the same bitstream utilising a hybrid of "reserved-slot" (c.f. TDM) and best effort (unreserved) resources in the switch nodes.

For the live production and presentation of audio, the proposed technology gives low latency performance as well as the support of multiplexed multiple channels each of which use different sampling rates and word lengths. The technology is also being considered for compressed media, including video.

Keywords: Low Latency · Packet Networks · Media Networking · Real Time Audio · Video

1 The Problem with Traditional IP-Based Media

There has been a *de facto* adoption of Internet Protocol (IP) equipment and networks in the vast majority of industries globally. This is partly understandable due to the ubiquity of IP which has led to increasing demand from customers, and increasing development and production of larger, more efficient and economic IP infrastructure from solution providers. Industries increasingly required a "commercial off-the-shelf" (COTS) range of solutions to support main operations from customer-facing offerings through to back-office services support.

D. Crawford et al. (Eds.): TIE 2023, LNICST 575, pp. 146–157, 2024.
https://doi.org/10.1007/978-3-031-59383-3_10

This is especially evident in the broadcast industry where the traditional SDI infrastructure had provided for a solid support of quality of service (QoS)-enabled media with real-time performance and negligible latency. But the drive towards IP has led to SMPTE (the Society of Motion Picture and Television Engineers) to introduce standards for media production over IP infrastructure in production facilities, resulting in the ST2022 and 2110 standards [2].

However, there is a major problem with the utilization of IP for real-time media. IP transport requires that the switching nodes at which media packets are routed have to buffer the individual packets, and then undertake examination and processing of the packet in order to establish which port and route the packet is to take in its forward journey through the network. This processing is a significant delay in the transport of the media. Over a network link, a media session may require as many as five to eight (or more) such routing "hops". The end-to-end latency results in the problems we all experience in "real time" online conference applications. For informal speech calls these delays can be tolerated as a compromise for the convenience of online meetings. However this is unworkable for real-time interaction, for example online music collaboration and other interactive services.

The issues arise across the network and in the main environments the signal encounters:

- media processing systems
- analogue/digital/analogue conversion
- digital consoles
- computer systems (e.g. with software plugins)

The current and recent established audio networking standards are given below.

2 Current and Recently Established Audio Networking Standards

AES 3 (commonly known as AES-EBU) is a digital audio interface which allows 2 channels of audio with status, clocking and control data [3]. AES10 can transport 56 or 64 channels of digital audio on a single link. The standard defines the serial MADI (Multichannel Audio Digital Interface) interface [1]. AES67 is the current standard for audio over IP and has been adopted in full in the SMPTE ST2110 standards for carriage of audio over IP in broadcast production [4, 5]. Audio video bridging (AVB) is an IEEE standard extension to the Ethernet standard to provide guaranteed quality of service with improved synchronization, low-latency, and reliability for switched Ethernet networks [6, 7]. Dante, developed by Audinate Pty. Ltd., provides a hardware and software solution for low latency transport of multi-channel digital audio over standard IP over an Ethernet network [8, 9].

The professional audio industry has been reluctant to use current Internet solutions for time critical applications. Live audio applications typically use networking technologies specifically designed for audio utilsing modified layer-2 or layer-3 (network layer) protocols. These applications have typically used EtherSound [10], CobraNet [11] etc. Current QoS solutions include traffic engineering and over-provisioning. It is generally perceived in the industry that these solutions complicate the system, increase power requirements and add cost.

The solution addressed in this paper focuses specifically on uncompressed audio, making use of its deterministic nature. However, the technology is equally applicable to video (including where low-latency compression is used) and other live media such as tactile. Next generation interactivity will allow viewers to interact with on-screen and second screen apps, including viewer-to-viewer interaction. This will require a highly responsive support of video traffic on carrier networks.

In conclusion, an architecture which supports time critical data simultaneously with best effort data is a difficult technical proposition. Architectures which support connectionless packet traffic are not inherently suited to support deterministic low latency data. Current multiplexing solutions are also unable to support flexible routing for multichannel streams which contain input streams with a range of sampling frequencies and variable bit lengths unless they undergo sample rate conversion and data reformatting.

Further to this, whilst the problem stated here has focused on media transport, there are other considerations for practical commercial networks. Such networks will carry a mix of time-sensitive media along with other data types which don't have the same latency constraints. This latter type of data is usually referred to as "best effort"; i.e. it is to be transmitted at the earliest opportune time for the network. Consequently the solution described here addresses the optimised routing of both types of traffic.

The time-deterministic media are denoted here as "synchronous data" (SF). The non-time-critical media are denoted here as "asynchronous data" (AF). A third data type is also identified here as Control Message (CM) data for the Flexilink session control and link management.

3 The Flexilink Solution

The Flexilink solution can be considered as combining the advantages of (i) a best effort packet network, and (ii) a Time Division Multiplex (TDM) link [12]. TDM technology is somewhat overlooked now: whilst the performance of TDM links provided for a reliable low latency transfer of constant timeslots, it was also wasteful on network resources due to the reservation of a constant network slot for each user-to-user link, whether there was any data to transfer or not. This resulted in a lot of waste of bandwidth in networks since much user session traffic carries no traffic (either because there is no data, or due to gaps in conversational speech. IP-based packets were therefore seen as the more economical solution for data and for audio traffic types. The Flexilink solution also aims to interwork compatibly with existing network protocols and infrastructure. The prototype implementation of Flexilink is achieved mainly through the "Aubergine" equipment units which provide the operational platform for each node.

For time-deterministic (Synchronous Flow, SF) data, we could consider the transmission of a traditional stereo (i.e. two channels) audio data sampled at 44.1 kHz with 16 bit samples. Discounting any headers or an error checking mechanism, this would require 1.4112Mb/s. So for a link with enough bandwidth there is sufficient information to assess and pre-allocate slots in the outbound bit stream for the data packets carrying the synchronous flow (SF) data.

Assuming ports exiting the switch will not be fully loaded with such data, there will be gaps between the SF data packets. These gaps can then be utilised for asynchronous

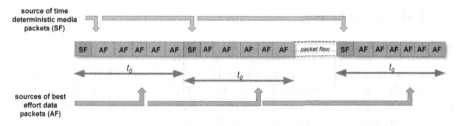

Fig. 1. A Link model: SF and AF packet allocation in the packet flow.

flow (AF) data. An idealised link model is illustrated in Fig. 1: SF data packets are shown as being transmitted at a constant time t_0. SF data packets will vary in length due to the nature of the incoming audio stream formats, and so the gaps between them will also be variable. These gaps will eventually be filled with the AF (asynchronous flow) data.

SF data needs to be transmitted in a time deterministic manner, so link resources for the outgoing link (i.e. bandwidth requirements) need to be assessed and reserved when the link is initially established. Each SF data packet can be identified by its position within the stream. This is a reliable identification and avoids bloated addressing additions to the data. This time-wise allocation of the link to SF data is somewhat similar to time slots as allocated in a TDM frame. Control messages (CM) are used by Flexilink nodes negotiating resource reservations and establishing network links.

Variable length SF packets are supported in the system; the gaps between these packets are therefore also variable and will be filled by AF traffic awaiting transmission. To enable this, a header is added to an SF packet. The header needs to contain only the SF packet length and basic error checking bits; the header is therefore kept to a minimal size so it doesn't inflate the transmitted data.

The AF stream may be considered as a byte stream that pauses when the real-time SF packets are transmitted. There is no need for AF data to be encapsulated with a new header when it is fragmented by the SF flow; this also simplifies the hardware logic required to forward both SF and AF traffic effectively.

There is no additional complex reassembly required to reconstruct the segmented AF traffic. In addition, this design can achieve the maximum utilization of link bandwidth with all the gaps (unused capacity) filled by the available best effort traffic. A similar process had been proposed in [13] and [14].

Layer 2 protocols defined in Flexilink have been developed along with a prototype network processor architecture and interface cards. These maintain compatibility with existing Ethernet infrastructure. Full-duplex mode operation is achieved (where non-deterministic CSMA-CD can be avoided).

4 Flexilink Operation

4.1 Flow Routing

Figure 2 shows an example of the operation: Three SFs are shown here with SF2 being multicast. Resources (i.e. bandwidth requirements) need to be reserved when the link is established to support deterministic media data. SF data packets are identified by their position in the stream (c.f. time slots in a TDM frame).

AFs are transmitted in available time in the frame not allocated to SF data.

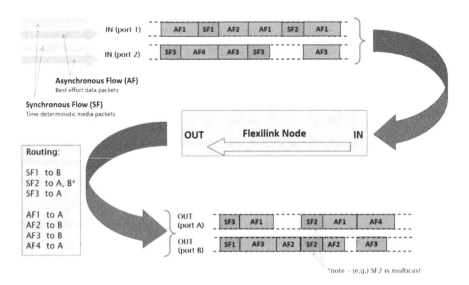

Fig. 2. Flexilink operation.

4.2 Flexilink Architecture in the Network Node

Figure 3 shows the architecture of the Flexilink network node (implemented in the Aubergine switch units). The network node supporting the proposed Flexilink would have a common network architecture with two major functional blocks:

- The "control unit" for setting up and tearing down call flows, allocating the resources, and route-finding algorithms.
- The data "forwarding logic" for fast forwarding and switching the data for both SF and AF data.

The initial process is for setting up and tearing down the link between two end points with an intelligent time slot map allocation algorithm. This is based on the available network link resources and the requirements of deterministic traffic (SF). This setup can be managed by control messages (CM).

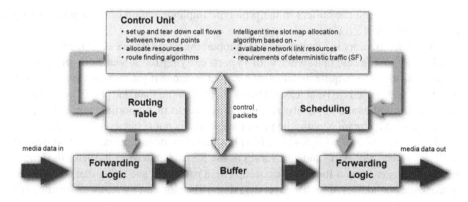

Fig. 3. Flexilink node Architecture.

The CM can be implemented using the messages and protocols specified in ETSI GS NIN 005 [15]. CMs are considered as normal AF traffic for the purposes of the link. Whereas AF traffic is routed to the output to be transmitted over the link, the CMs are directed to the controller. CMs have priority over AFs on each link.

p = parity; f=flag (which can be used to show end of message)

Fig. 4. Synchronous Flow (SF) Packet Format.

Figure 4 shows the simplified packet headers. The simple header added to SFs contain only the length information.

The header consists of: 6 bits to encode the length information; 1 bit parity; and a 1-bit flag which the upper layers can use to assist reassembly into larger data units if required.

4.3 Slots and SF Packets

Originally it was intended that SF packets could be any length, from two or three bytes to hold a single audio sample to several kilobytes to hold an uncompressed video picture line. However, it is not easy for a flow needing frequent small transmission slots to share a link with one needing very large slots. For instance, on a 1 Gb/s link a 4 KB slot would occupy the link for 32 μs. If slots have already been allocated every 10.4 μs for a 96 kHz audio flow, some of those slots will need to be moved, adding to the latency of the audio and probably also requiring slots on downstream links to be moved also. Switches would need bigger buffers; the buffers in the prototype implementation only support holding packets for about 15 μs.

The buffer memory in a switch needs to support the total data rate of all the interfaces, e.g. 480 Gb/s in the case of a switch with 48 ports carrying 10 Gb/s each. In practice this means it needs to have quite a wide data path, for instance if the memory interface is at 1 GHz the width needs to be at least 60 bytes. Routing more than one packet per memory cycle adds significant complexity, so there is no benefit in supporting very small slots provided the AF stream can use the part of a slot that is not occupied by a packet.

A fixed slot size of 64 bytes (512 bits) has therefore been chosen. The first byte of each slot is the "slot start" and also serves as the SF packet header; it carries the length of the SF packet (zero if the slot is unoccupied), a parity bit, and a flag that can be used to mark the boundaries of higher-layer data units. The slot start bytes are an overhead of less than 1.6% on the wire, and there is no additional overhead for SF packet headers. Using a fixed slot size avoids needing a protocol for the transmitter to tell the receiver where the slots are located.

If this seems very similar to ATM's AAL5 it should be remembered that unused space in the slot is not wasted but is available to the AF stream. Moreover, traditional packet data does not need to be segmented (or "shredded") - the AF packet format provides efficient support for lengths from 1 to 2000 bytes. It is only the real-time data that needs to be segmented; it is a continuous stream, so will require segmentation whatever the packet size, and smaller packets take less time to fill, thus minimising the packetisation delay.

4.4   Interface Architecture

Ideally, for maximum compatibility, Flexilink should be able to use the existing physical network interface. However to support the proposed Flexilink protocol, a new media access control (MAC) layer architecture needs to be considered, which allows AF and SF to be treated differently.

AF and SF have separate buffers and copy-logic allocated for them. The SF input has a 15 μs buffer from which the packets are taken to fill the output slots. Multicasting can easily be achieved simply by copying the same packet to several different outputs (Fig. 5).

The SF buffer, containing the last 15 μs of data from each input, is small enough to go in internal block RAM in the FPGA. The larger AF buffer is in external dRAM, and contains one queue per output.

4.5   Supporting Flexible Multichannel Audio Streams with Different Sampling Frequencies

The current problem in networking audio traffic is the lack of flexibility to support arbitrary numbers of audio channels with different sampling frequencies and of compressed or uncompressed data format. In Flexilink multiple channels of different sampling frequencies can be readily supported as long as the link capacity is sufficient.

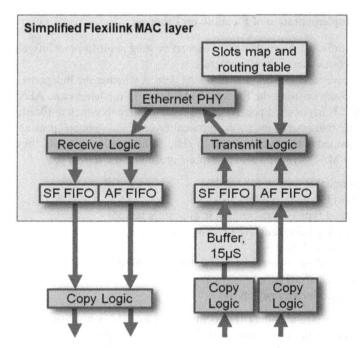

Fig. 5.   Interface architecture to support Flexilink.

The control message that requests setting up a flow from a media source to an output includes the number of slots required per second. It also includes a specification of the format, though that is only used by the end-systems, not by the network.

The network allocates the required slots on each link the flow traverses. Frames on each link are phase-locked so that the delay through each switch is constant (within a small tolerance window); the alignment mechanism does not require any clocks to be synchronized.

Audio in the prototype implementation uses a "transparent AES3" format to send up to 7 stereo samples occupying 8 bytes each. There is an additional 1 byte per packet that encodes a timestamp. For 44.1 and 48 kHz sampling 8000 slots per second are used, and at the source the incoming samples are accumulated until it is time for the packet to be transmitted; this results in typically 5 or 6 samples in a packet. This process is simple enough that it can be implemented in hardware (in the prototypes it is handled by the FPGA), removing the need for processing by software.

The system also distributes time to a similar accuracy to Precision Time Protocol; this can be used to distribute a "house clock". Audio output clocks can also be adjusted to match the rate of arrival of audio samples over the network; this is made easier by the absence of jitter in arrival times.

4.6 The Implementation of Flexilink on Ethernet

SF and AF traffic can be implemented over an existing point-to-point link, and so is able to utilise a current network infrastructure.

The receive-side network interface auto-detects whether the link partner is sending Flexilink frames or using the Ethernet MAC layer. In the latter case, AES51 [add ref, also for AES3] negotiation packets can be used to agree to switch to Flexilink mode.

Flexilink frames are seen by the physical layer ICs as "jumbo" packets 7793 bytes long, transmitted at a nominal rate of 16 kHz. To minimize overheads, they omit all of the Ethernet MAC layer and also part of the preamble; the format is:

- 2 bytesPreamble
- 1 byteStart Frame Delimiter (SFD)
- 1 byteFrame type (shows position in allocation period)
- 4 bytesTiming information (PTP-compatible)
- 7744 bytes121 slots
- 40 bytes"Trailing" bytes (less than a slot; carry AF data)
- 4 bytesLongitudinal parity
- 12 to 18 bytesInterframe gap (IFG)

Total frame size including IFG is thus 7808 to 7814 bytes. One unit is chosen as the reference for the frame rate, and the size of the gap on each link is adjusted to keep the phase relationship constant. An average gap of 16.5 bytes corresponds to the nominal 16 kHz, so two frames take 125 μS, the same period as used in the Synchronous Digital Hierarchy (SDH), Firewire, full speed USB, etc. An average of 14 corresponds to 16.005 kHz which ensures that (assuming no excessive tolerances) there will always be at least the requested number of slots, even if the source's clock is faster than nominal and the network's is slower.

The longitudinal parity is used to monitor link quality, as in SDH; it is simpler to implement than the Ethernet Frame Check Sequence, and by being different ensures that frames will not be interpreted as Ethernet packets. Routing of incoming packets does not require the FCS has been received, which would require additional buffering and delays. Instead, application-specific end-to-end check sequences are used as appropriate; for many media formats it is better to deliver data with a few bit errors than to discard whole packets.

The framing does not play any part in the interpretation of the AF stream, beyond specifying which of the incoming bytes are part of it. SF packets are identified by their position in the frame and the position of the frame in the allocation period (indicated by the frame type byte) (i.e. t1 for SF1, t2 for SF2, etc.) Consequently labels for identification of SF flows are not required.

4.7 Hardware Implementation

The Flexilink architecture needs to be implemented on various network devices such as single port or multi-port interface cards, and switches. The main functions on these devices are the data forwarding unit and the control unit.

The incoming AF stream on each port is written to a FIFO from which packets are copied to a buffer in dRAM. The packet header includes a label which selects an entry in a routing table that shows the port on which it is to be output and the label for the next hop; for each port there is a single queue of AF packets to be output. Note that a packet is not routed until it has completely arrived, to prevent other inputs being blocked from writing to the same queue, and that it is not possible to predict how long that will take because it depends on how much space is taken up by SF packets. Control messages are carried on a flow that is routed to a queue from which they are taken by the control unit.

All incoming SF packets are written to a circular buffer which is small enough to be held in sRAM. There is a routing table for each output, showing the location to be read in the buffer for each outgoing slot. Note that whereas the AF routing table for each port is on the input, the SF routing table is on the output (Fig. 6).

Fig. 6. Four Aubergine units

The routing tables are written by the control unit, to connect and disconnect flows. Note that the forwarding of packets (both AF and SF) is done entirely by hardware logic. The control unit allocates network resources for multichannel SF data requests and achieves this by positioning the SF data packet in the continuous bit stream on an outgoing port appropriate for the route required. SF data packets are allocated evenly to allow phase correction algorithms to work efficiently. The control unit needs to be an effective general-purpose CPU with accelerated networking processing capabilities.

Prototype units that can act both as a network switch and as an interface for digital audio and video have been built on a platform consisting of a Xilinx XC6SLX45T FPGA, dRAM, flash memory, and physical interfaces; this was developed and built at Nine Tiles Networks Ltd. The processor is implemented in the FPGA fabric. The high-level language in which it is programmed is optimised for processing protocol messages.

5 Interconnection with Existing Network Technologies

A mixed network environment will have multiple low latency audio flows of different sampling frequencies, bit depths and numbers of channels. This can be supported by Flexilink technology as described above. Normal data transfer, typically IP-based traffic (e.g. file transfer), is mapped into the AF traffic and can be transmitted over a Flexilink network.

The architecture design maintains separation between the AF and SF data. This ensures that there is no interference between two types of data whilst utilizing the bandwidth not used by SF data for AF data.

For IP based audio, Flexilink can map audio IP packets to SF data packets according to the identified service priority. Flexilink should not negate the original QoS requirements. In the case where a Flexilink interface is peering with a normal Ethernet interface, the Ethernet MAC must be used. The Flexilink unit can either (i) encapsulate the Ethernet packets in an AF flow or (ii) extract the audio from the Ethernet packets and re-pack it as an SF flow. The latter will give lower latency and allow the flow to be connected to native Flexilink audio interfaces.

6 Future Work and Impact

Flexilink can be a good candidate layer 2 technology to support guaranteed QoS for upper layer applications, for example synchronized audio/video delivery and low latency interactive media distribution networks. The Flexilink network architecture also provides a solution for QoS guaranteed end-to-end Integrated Service. Development is currently addressing scalability, interoperability, and security. The technology is also being evaluated for proposed application to current network issues including next generation (6G) mobile access.

References

1. AES, AES10-2020: AES Recommended Practice for Digital Audio Engineering - Serial Multichannel Audio Digital Interface (MADI). https://www.aes.org/publications/standards/search.cfm?docID=17. Accessed 09 Jun 2023
2. Lavoie, R.: Introduction to ST 2022-6 & ST 2110. https://www.riedel.net/fileadmin/user_upload/800-downloads/07-Guides/White_Paper_-_ST_2022-6_vs_ST_2110_final.pdf. Accessed 09 Jun 2023
3. EBU, Specification of the Digital Audio Interface (The AES/EBU interface) Tech. 3250-E - Third edition 2004. https://tech.ebu.ch/docs/tech/tech3250.pdf. Accessed 09 Jun 2023
4. SMPTE, ST 2110 Suite of Standards. https://www.smpte.org/standards/st2110. Accessed 09 Jun 2023
5. Cardinal Peak. Introduction to AES67. https://www.cardinalpeak.com/blog/intro-to-aes67. Accessed 09 Jun 2023
6. Presonus, An Introduction to AVB Networking. https://legacy.presonus.com/learn/technical-articles/an-introduction-to-avb-networking. Accessed 09 Jun 2023
7. IEEE802.org, 802.1BA - Audio Video Bridging (AVB) Systems. https://www.ieee802.org/1/pages/802.1ba.html. Accessed 09 Jun 2023

8. Audinate. https://www.audinate.com/meet-dante/what-is-dante. Accessed 09 Jun 2023
9. Canford. DANTE networking basics. https://www.canford.co.uk/TechZone/Article/DANTE. Accessed 09 Jun 2023
10. Allen & Heath, EtherSound OVERVIEW. https://www.allen-heath.com/ahproducts/ethersound. Accessed 09 Jun 2023
11. Cobranet. https://www.cobranet.info/. Accessed 09 Jun 2023
12. Wat Electronics. What is Time Division Multiplexing: Working & Its Applications, https://www.watelectronics.com/time-division-multiplexing. Accessed 09 Jun 2023
13. Froggatt, D.: Data Transmission System, 22-Jan-1986 (1986)
14. Strong, P., Wild, T., Dean, G.: Latency reduction by adaptive packet fragmentation, 07-Mar-2008 (2008)
15. ETSI, ETSI GS NIN 005 V1.1.1 (2022–11), Non-IP Networking (NIN); Signalling messages and protocols. https://www.etsi.org/deliver/etsi_gs/NIN/001_099/005/01.01.01_60/gs_NIN005v010101p.pdf. Accessed 09 Jun 2023

Author Index

Printed in the United States
by Baker & Taylor Publisher Services